Wreck, Boat and Drift Diving

by

Steven M. Barsky

SCUBA DIVING INTERNATIONAL

Published by
Scuba Diving International
Topsham, Maine

Wreck, Boat and Drift Diving
by Steven M. Barsky

Scuba Diving International
18 Elm Street
Topsham, ME 04086
Tel: 207-729-4201
FAX: 207-729-4453

Find us on the World Wide Web at http://www.tdisdi.com/

Photography
Principal photography by Bret Gilliam. ©Bret Gilliam. All rights reserved. Additional photography © Steven M. Barsky, Kristine Barsky, and Wayne Hasson.

Primary photo models: Skip Dunham, Lynn Hendrickson, Cathryn Castle, Lina Hitchcock, Gretchen Gilliam, Tom Burgener, Sarah Humphries, Brian Stephensen, Kristine Barsky, and Scott Lockwood.

Illustrations:
© Steven M. Barsky. All rights reserved.

Printed by Ojai Printing, Ojai, CA

ISBN Number:1-931451-04-4

Library of Congress Control Number: 2002103967

Other Titles Available from Scuba Diving International

Training Manual for Scuba Diving: Dive Training for the 21st Century
Easy Nitrox Diving
Night Diving, Underwater Navigation, and Limited Visibility Diving
Deeper Sport Diving with Dive Computers
Rescue Diving Manual: A Guide to Rescue Techniques, Stress, Injury, and Accident Management
Dry Suit Diving
Solo Diving Techniques: A Manual for Independent Diving Skills
Visual Inspection Procedures: A Manual for Cylinder Safety
CPROX: Guidelines for Essential CPR and Oxygen Administration
CPR-1st: A Concise Manual for Emergency First Aid and CPR

Other Titles Available from Technical Diving International

Nitrox Diver Manual
Advanced Nitrox Diver Manual
Decompression Procedures Manual
Semi-Closed Circuit Rebreather Manual: Draeger Units
Trimix Diving Manual
Extended Range Diver Manual
Cave and Cavern Diving Manual
Advanced Wreck Diving
Deep Diving: An Advanced Guide to Physiology, Procedures, and Systems
Nitrox Blending Manual: Guide to Preparation of Oxygen Enriched Air
Advanced Gas Blending Manual: Nitrox, Trimix, and Custom Mixes
Equipment Service Tech Manual

WARNING

The underwater activities described in this book expose the diver to unique risks, as well as risks common to all underwater recreation, such as drowning,

The risks that are commonly encountered in wreck diving include entanglement in fishing lines and nets, accidental wreck penetration and entrapment in a wreck, cuts from sharp metal, explosions caused by undetonated ordnance aboard military wrecks, and disorientation due to compass errors. If the diver has inadequate training or fails to follow correct procedures, these risks can result in serious injury or death.

Boat diving presents another set of risks that must be considered by divers who participate in diving activities conducted from vessels. The risks that may be encountered during boat diving include being swept away by a strong current, being left behind at a remote dive site by a boat operator, being struck by the boat while in the water, or having the boat sink while aboard. These risks can also cause serious injury or death.

Drift diving presents its own set of challenges and risks for the diver. Strong currents can cause a diver to become lost at sea. Down draft currents can push a diver deeper than planned. Both of these hazards can cause serious injury or death.

Table of Contents

Table of Contents

sels have provided divers with the most intriguing wreck diving sites. These ships are better able to withstand the ravages of time and in many cases can survive over a hundred years of entombment while remaining virtually intact. A classic example is the wreck of the Royal Mail Steamer Rhone sunk in 1867 off Salt Island in the British Virgin Islands. Although her stern section sank in 15 to 45 feet of water and has been largely reduced to rubble and scattered wreckage by over 135 years of pounding surf and currents, her massive bow section (nearly 200 feet long) remains fully intact in 90 foot depths resting on her starboard side. The Rhone has become the most popular wreck dive in the eastern Caribbean and much of the movie *The Deep* was shot using her remains as a natural set in 1976.

The east coast of the United States has been blessed with a wide variety of wrecks that have remained accessible due to the relatively shallow offshore continental shelf. A proverbial grab bag of ages, types, sizes and degrees of difficulty are offered to divers of all levels from Key West, Florida to Eastport, Maine. Some of the best sites resulted from sinkings during the two World Wars when many a tanker, freighter, or war ship fell victim to submarine attack. Similar wreck sites are widely available around the coasts of England, Ireland, and many areas of Europe.

Some of the best wreck diving in the world can found in areas of the Pacific such as Truk Lagoon in the small country of Chuuk, part of the Federated States of Micronesia. Within the protected waters of the natural atoll lie the hulks of over a hundred merchant and war ships in depths easily accessible to sport divers.

Today divers are not limited just to natural wrecks. The popularity of creating artificial reefs by using surplus naval vessels and ships that have outlived their commercial usefulness is increasing. In the fall of 1993 the city of Miami even sponsored a commercial jet airliner as the latest addition to the scores of deliberately placed wrecks off the south Florida coastline. Originally the push for artificial reef projects was fueled by fishing interests. Charter fishing captains had known for years the value of wrecks to attract and become home to resident fish populations. As divers began to visit these same sites, a symbiotic dual use was realized.

The economic value of sinking surplus vessels as diving attractions has now grown in popularity and a cornucopia of wrecks of all types and sizes have now been re-cycled off the East, West and Gulf coasts of the U.S., Canada, the Bahamas, the Cayman Islands, the British Virgin Islands, and literally countless other regions where divers come to enjoy their ever-expanding resources.

This book will explain how to visit these sites safely and with the prop-

Foreword by Bret Gilliam

President and CEO
Scuba Diving International

Probably the first motivation for people to attempt diving was in the pursuit of shipwrecks, either for commercial salvage purposes or to recover sunken cargoes that included classic treasure riches. And while there are countless interesting subjects to keep us enthralled underwater, the chance to explore a shipwreck, no matter how small or deteriorated, holds a special spot in the hearts of all divers.

Most people have a romantic image of the sunken treasure ship sitting upright on her keel with tattered sails still creaking in the current and brass bound chests straining with booty. Well, reality is a bit less dramatic. The classic 16th and 17th century vessels sailing to the New World laden with riches were, of course, of wooden construction. Once sunk they quickly deteriorated due to wave action and other natural elements such as destructive marine teredo worms which fed on the primary wood structure.

Those who have been successful in locating and salvaging these vessels have usually spent years researching logs and voyage records to determine the wreck location. Since the wrecks themselves were long buried under sand or coral there was typically no evidence to the diver's naked eye of a lost vessel. Tedious excavation of tons of sand, sediment, and debris was necessary before any cargo could be accessed. As diving wrecks, these older ships offered little in the way of interest unless one was a committed treasure hunter with a considerable war chest of funding. Even then your odds of success were better in the state lottery.

Although some modern wooden ships are remarkably well preserved in fresh water environments such as the Great Lakes, as a general rule steel ves-

scattered wreckage by over 135 years of pounding surf and currents, her massive bow section (nearly 200 feet long) remains fully intact in 90 foot depths resting on her starboard side. The Rhone has become the most popular wreck dive in the eastern Caribbean and much of the movie *The Deep* was shot using her remains as a natural set in 1976.

The east coast of the United States has been blessed with a wide variety of wrecks that have remained accessible due to the relatively shallow offshore continental shelf. A proverbial grab bag of ages, types, sizes and degrees of difficulty are offered to divers of all levels from Key West, Florida to Eastport, Maine. Some of the best sites resulted from sinkings during the two World Wars when many a tanker, freighter, or war ship fell victim to submarine attack. Similar wreck sites are widely available around the coasts of England, Ireland, and many areas of Europe.

Some of the best wreck diving in the world can found in areas of the Pacific such as Truk Lagoon in the small country of Chuuk, part of the Federated States of Micronesia. Within the protected waters of the natural atoll lie the hulks of over a hundred merchant and war ships in depths easily accessible to sport divers.

Today divers are not limited just to natural wrecks. The popularity of creating artificial reefs by using surplus naval vessels and ships that have outlived their commercial usefulness is increasing. In the fall of 1993 the city of Miami even sponsored a commercial jet airliner as the latest addition to the scores of deliberately placed wrecks off the south Florida coastline. Originally the push for artificial reef projects was fueled by fishing interests. Charter fishing captains had known for years the value of wrecks to attract and become home to resident fish populations. As divers began to visit these same sites, a symbiotic dual use was realized.

The economic value of sinking surplus vessels as diving attractions has now grown in popularity and a cornucopia of wrecks of all types and sizes have now been re-cycled off the East, West and Gulf coasts of the U.S., Canada, the Bahamas, the Cayman Islands, the British Virgin Islands, and literally countless other regions where divers come to enjoy their ever-expanding resources.

This book will explain how to visit these sites safely and with the proper diving practices. While many texts treat wreck diving as a singular subject, the practical reality suggests that we combine this subject with material on boat diving since the best wrecks are usually accessed only by boat. In addition to wrecks, boat diving opens up a far wider spectrum of diving opportunities than would be available if limited only to swimming from shore as independent divers.

er diving practices. While many texts treat wreck diving as a singular subject, the practical reality suggests that we combine this subject with material on boat diving since the best wrecks are usually accessed only by boat. In addition to wrecks, boat diving opens up a far wider spectrum of diving opportunities than would be available if limited only to swimming from shore as independent divers.

This text will cover in considerable detail all the elements of diving from both commercial charter vessels and private craft. Everything from how to stow your gear to applicable local and government regulations is discussed along with valuable explanations of methodology and etiquette. And since many sites require divers to deal with currents, we have incorporated special instructions on drift diving practices as well.

You'll find this text to be a valuable resource on an exciting subject. We've enjoyed putting it together and hope you'll enjoy the wonderful benefits of boat diving and the exploration of wrecks as much as we have. Good diving!

Bret Gilliam
President and CEO TDI/SDI

Acknowledgements

Of all the diving that I do, I would have to say that wreck diving is one of my favorite activities. When I can combine wreck diving with underwater photography, I am truly in a state of bliss. And, when I can dive a great wreck from my own boat, it is a an even more special adventure.

I've had the good fortune to dive wrecks all over the world, including the wreck of the Arizona in Pearl Harbor, with the National Park Service. Whether it's been a tramp steamer in the Caribbean, a submarine off Hawaii, or a steamship off California, wreck diving always gets my blood boiling!

The experiences, tips, and techniques in this book are the result of many years of diving with special friends in some unique settings. Two of the divers who are featured in this book have been with me on some of my most special dives; most notably my friend, Skip Dunham, and my wife Kristine. I owe both of them a special "thank-you" for their help in creating many of the photos you will see here.

As with all of my books, I find myself grateful for the assistance and cooperation of many people.

- Harry Averill with Dive-Rite
- Wayne Hasson - Aggressor Fleet
- David Crockford at SDI/TDI HQ in England
- John Wall at The Dive Shop, Fairfax, Virginia
- Dan Ruth and Brian Stevenson at Live/Dive Pacific
- Lynn Hendrickson, Brian Carney, and Sean Harrison at TDI/SDI Headquarters

I hope that you enjoy wreck diving as much as I do, and perhaps we'll get to meet some day on a dive boat and share a dive.

Steve Barsky
Ventura, California

Chapter 1
Exploring Shipwrecks and Other Boat Diving Adventures

Many divers think that wreck diving is the most exciting underwater activity that you can pursue. Whether you are exploring the liberty ships or submarines off the east coast of the U.S., the WWI German fleet off Scapa Flow in England, "wreck alley" off San Diego, or the galleons off the Florida keys, there's something about shipwrecks that stirs most divers into a frenzy. Perhaps it's the thought of finding sunken "treasure," the chance to photograph the guns on a warship, or the beauty of a wreck as it slowly becomes an artificial reef that lures you.

Shipwrecks are bits of history, frozen time capsules of the era they sailed on the day the ship went down. To explore a shipwreck is to learn about the past. Once you visit a wreck, you'll almost always want to know more about it. Or, you may learn about an undiscovered wreck and research it to locate it for diving.

The wreck of the Royal Mail Steamship Rhone is an example of a classic shipwreck and one of the most picturesque that you can explore. She sank in 1867 in a violent hurricane that ripped through the British Virgin Islands. The huge open end wrenches used to work on her engine are still in place, as are the cannons used to defend her. You can see the crow's nest, the mast, and many other parts of the engine and ship's fittings.

As you become involved with shipwreck diving, you'll undoubtedly want to know why each wreck sank, how it sank, and when it sank. The stories behind wrecks are almost always fascinating to discover!

Shipwrecks are great places to see marine life, because they provide hiding places and opportunities for both small and large marine creatures. Lobsters can be found inside ship's cabins, under deck plates, and inside masts and pipes. Barracuda swirl around tropical wrecks. Tiny fish known as "glassy sweepers" school by the thousands inside warm water wrecks around the

The wreck of the Rhone in the British Virgin Islands is one of the most picturesque shipwrecks in the world. It looks almost exactly like most people would imagine a shipwreck should look. In the mid-70's it was used to film the movie, "The Deep."

world. Soft corals wrap their tentacles around the railings of old freighters and spiny oysters grow on any available surface. Yet, the shape of the wreck can still be seen beneath these mantles of living creatures.

For underwater photographers, shipwrecks present an infinite variety of photographic opportunities, whether you want to shoot macro close-ups or wide angle. You can capture images of tiny, colorful starfish living on the hull of a ship, or frame a diver swimming examining a giant ship's propeller. If you shoot video, your viewers can make a "virtual" dive by watching your explorations on tape or computer.

Many of the best dive sites are accessible only by boat

Many of the best shipwrecks in the world are accessible only by boat. In most cases, this is true because the more interesting wrecks are usually in deeper water, a good distance from shore. When wrecks sink in deep water, they are protected from the ravages of waves and surf, that break shallow water wrecks into bits and pieces. For this reason, if you're serious about wreck diving, you'll undoubtedly find that many of your dives take place from boats.

You will usually find more marine life at remote dive sites. These lobsters were taken at Santa Cruz Island, off the coast of California.

Boats like the Okeanos Aggressor are ideal for long-range exploration of remote dive sites. This vessel makes regular trips to Cocos Island, off the coast of Central America.

Boat diving is in most cases, the most convenient and easy way to dive. You don't have to hike down a cliff or climb over rocks to get to the water.You don't have to clean sand off your equipment after diving. You don't have to contend with surf, and usually the visibility offshore is much better than it is near shore. There's usually a place to change into your bathing suit or back into your clothes.

Boat diving encompasses many different types of vessels, any of which can provide enjoyable adventures. Small boats(under 28 feet/8.5 metres in length) can be used to take you to almost any coastal locations, but usually not more than 50 miles (80 kilometres) offshore. Larger vessels have the capability of visiting remote locations that may be as much as a day or more from port.

Drift dives are almost always conducted by boat

In many parts of the world, there are strong currents that flow through exotic dive sites, providing an almost effortless type of diving experience. In these situations, the diver is carried along by a "river" of water in the ocean, on a rapid trip with underwater sights whizzing by. The dive starts in one location and ends up at what may be a considerable distance downstream from the original location.

On a drift dive, the usual procedure is for divers to submerge as part of a group, lead by a divemaster. The divemaster carries a line attached to a surface float. The group drifts along with the current and the dive boat (or a smaller chase boat) follows the divemaster's float. In an area with strong currents, drift divers can cover an enormous amount of territory in a vert short period of time.

Drift dives can be conducted in almost any part of the world and each drift dive is usually a unique and unusual experience. For example, Cozumel is known for its drift diving, as is the island of Tobago in the lower Caribbean. West Palm Beach, Florida has great drift diving as do many locations in the Pacific Northwest.

Drift diving is not for the novice diver. On a drift dive, it is usually difficult or impossible to stop at any one spot for any length of time. If you have any type of problem during a drift dive, you must be able to work it out as the current carries you along. Drift divers must also have excellent buoyancy control.

Shipwrecks are very photogenic subjects.

What will you learn during this course?

This course will be broken up into modules that may combine different elements, or may be taught separately, depending on the instructor, your interests, and where you live.

Since boat diving is central to this course, whether you plan to engage in drift diving or wreck diving, we'll start out by covering boat diving information. During this course you may have the opportunity to dive from both small and large boats.

During the boat diving module, you will be introduced to information that includes:

- Diving equipment for boat diving

- Boating accessories for diving
- Diving techniques for small boats
- Diving techniques for large boats
- Boat diving etiquette
- Boat diving safety

During the wreck diving module, you will learn to participate in "non-penetration wreck dives." A penetration dive is one where you enter the enclosed interior of the wreck, beyond the point where the wreck is illuminated by sunlight. This requires additional specialized equipment and training beyond what will be taught during this course. A non-penetration wreck dive is made solely on the exterior of the wreck. On most wrecks, there is plenty to see and explore without penetrating the wreck's interior.

During the wreck diving module, you will learn the following:

- Equipment selection for wreck diving
- Risks of wreck diving
- Where and how to research shipwrecks
- Planning wreck dives
- Techniques for wreck diving

In the drift diving module, we'll cover the general principles of drift diving that you can use no matter where you dive. Information specific to drift diving will include:

- Equipment for drift diving
- Procedures for drift diving
- Risks in drift diving
- Emergency procedures for drift diving

What will you be qualified to do when you complete this course?

Depending on the open water modules you complete – i.e., boat diving, wreck diving, and/or drift diving, you'll be qualified to participate in the following diving activities at the completion of this course:

- Participate in non-penetration wreck dives in open water at depths and under conditions similar to those in which you have trained.
- Participate in diving from a boat
- Participate in drift dives at depths and under conditions similar to those in which you have trained.

Scuba IQ Review

Do you expect to experience adventures during this course? You should, because the opportunities for underwater adventures are at their peak during wreck, boat, and drift dives! Discuss your expectations with your instructor as you review the questions below.

1) Explain the difference between "penetration" and "non-penetration" wreck dives.

2) List one reason why many wreck dives are done using a boat as a dive support platform.

3) Define the term "drift dive."

Notes:

Chapter 2 Preparing for Boat Diving

Like any specialized outdoor activity, boat diving requires some additional equipment beyond ordinary diving gear. The more remote the diving operation, the greater the need will be for specialized accessories.

If you are operating your own small boat, or joining a friend aboard their boat, you'll need to be more concerned and involved to ensure that everything that's needed to help ensure safety is aboard. If you're diving from a charter vessel that's licensed by the Coast Guard, you can usually be certain that the necessary safety gear is on board, but it still won't hurt to ask the crew what equipment they have on hand. If you personally charter a vessel, be it large or small, you want to ensure that the right equipment is on board.

Items that are considered essential for boat diving include a diver's flag, a current line, a marine VHF radio, a ladder, and an oxygen system. Additional items that will make your personal boat diving experience more enjoyable and safer include surface signaling devices, dry bags and boxes for your personal gear, hang-off lines for equipment, and underwater navigation systems.

We'll also deal with issues that are important to consider when you're planning for a boat dive. As you might expect, there are different levels of planning that you'll need to consider depending on who is running the boat.

Gear for Boat Diving

Boat diving accessories and equipment fall into two categories, accessories for the boat and personal accessories. Both types of gear are important to an enjoyable dive and to enhance your safety.

Some equipment may be provided by the people who operate the boat, while other items will be your responsibility.

The sport diving flag is used to alert other boat operators that there are divers in the water near your boat.

Diver's Down Flag

Every dive boat must fly a diver's down flag while divers are in the water to warn boat operators to stay clear of the area immediately surrounding the boat. The flag is a message to boat operators to stay away from the dive boat and be cautious in passing it.

Although every diver is familiar with the red and white diver's flag, not all boat operators know what it means. The problem is further compounded by the fact that the flag is not required by U.S. Coast Guard regulations, although many state and local laws require the use of the dive flag. Despite the widespread use of the dive flag, there have been numerous accidents where divers have been injured or killed by ignorant or careless boat operators. For this reason, you should always try to surface as close as possible to the boat from which you are diving.

The dive flag should be displayed from the highest point possible on the boat where it can be clearly seen from all directions. There are many accessories for mounting diver's flags, and these can be obtained from most boating supply stores.

Current Line

Whenever you are diving from a boat, especially at a location that is distant from shore, it is essential to have a current line. A current line is a length of floating line, usually yellow polypropylene, with a float attached to the end of it. Most current lines are usually a minimum of 100 feet (30 metres) in length, although they may be longer.

The current line is normally attached to the stern of the dive boat and is extended to its full length out behind the boat. The line is available to any diver who accidentally surfaces behind the boat and needs to pull themselves back to the boat if there is a current that is too strong to swim against.

The current line can be coiled into a basket or nylon mesh bag for storage. It's important to always remember to pull the current line back into the boat once all of the divers are back aboard to avoid tangling the line in the propeller.

Drift Diving Line and Float

Depending on sea conditions, depth, and other environmental factors, many divemasters will use a drift diving line and float to enable the boat to follow the divers on the bottom.

The Alpha Flag (Flag Alpha in Europe)

The alpha flag is another type of dive flag. It is the only one that is recognized under international maritime law. According to the Navigation Rules, International Inland, "whenever the size of a vessel engaged in diving operations makes it impracticable to exhibit all (warning) lights and shapes (normally required on larger vessels) the vessel will "exhibit a rigid International Code flag "A" not less than 1 meter in height."

The Alpha flag is a blue and white flag with an unusual shape. Most large dive boats will fly both the alpha flag and the red and white diver's flag. The Alpha flag is actually more appropriate to commercial diving operations than to sport diving operations, although sport diving charter vessels have increasingly used it in the U.S.

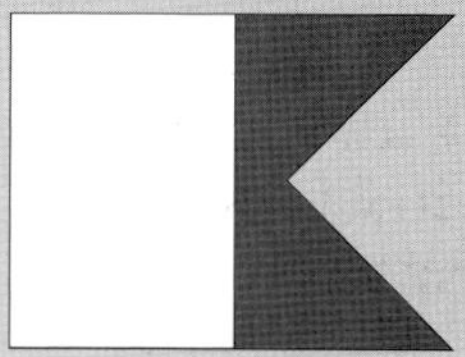

In the U.K., the use of the Flag Alpha is mandatory for <u>all</u> underwater operations.

It's always a good idea to use a current line when conducting diving operations from a dive boat in the ocean.

VHF Marine Radio

A VHF radio is your lifeline to the world whenever you're out aboard a boat. The radio provides communications with other boats in your area as well as emergency communications in the event of any diving or boating mishap.

Although many people today carry a cellular phone with them when they go to sea, a cell phone is not a good choice for emergency communications for several reasons. Cell phone coverage is not reliable in all areas and there are many "dead" zones, particularly behind rocky islands. Secondly, there may be boats that are close by that can lend assistance that you are unable to see, but that can hear your distress call if it goes out on a radio. If you only have a cell phone, there is no way that they will know that you need help. Finally, when you call for help on a marine radio, the Coast Guard can get an approximate fix on your location, even if you don't know your exact position.

VHF radios are available as compact hand-held units that are ideal for smaller boats, or as more powerful fixed-mount units with large antennas that will transmit over a longer range. You do not need a license to own or operate a VHF marine radio on a small, privately owned vessel, but you must follow correct radio operations procedures and etiquette. The Federal Communications Commission (FCC) can levy fines on boat operators who do not follow the rules for proper radio usage.

Using a VHF Radio

Boat operators are encouraged to monitor Channel 16 at all times while operating their vessel. Channel 16 may be used to hail other boats, but the main purpose for this channel is to provide for emergency radio traffic. All maritime authorities, like the U.S. Coast Guard and harbor police, monitor Channel 16 continuously. If you call another vessel on Channel 16, once you have established contact you must switch to another channel, such as 68. If you continue to have an ordinary conversation on Channel 16 you can be fined.

To call another vessel, you simply key the microphone and say something like, "Deep Diver, Deep Diver, this is the Blue Wave. Are you there?" Once you get a response you switch to another channel and resume your conversation.

Make sure that there is no one else talking on the channel you select before you start to transmit. Make each transmission short. At the end of each transmission, say the word "over," so that the person listening knows that you are done speaking for the moment.

When you have completed your conversation, say, "This is the Blue Wave (or whatever your boat's name is) clear on channel 68."

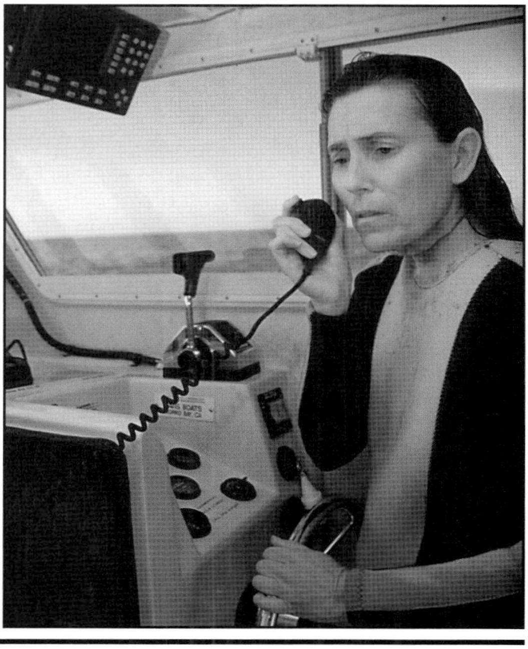

If you use a VHF radio, you must follow the proper procedures for its operation.

Oxygen System

Every dive boat should be equipped with an oxygen system, and the further you are from shore, the more oxygen you should carry with you. When you're out on a boat, there's no way for an ambulance to drive up to your location. Even at locations like Catalina Island, it takes time to mobilize a Coast Guard helicopter or the Baywatch lifeguards.

There should be sufficient oxygen aboard to make it from your most remote dive site back to shore. Oxygen is crucial in providing first aid for cases of decompression sickness and lung over-pressure injuries. There are now special kits that make it possible to reuse the onboard oxygen and extend its capability for many hours by removing the carbon dioxide generated each time you exhale. These systems function in a manner similar to a closed circuit rebreather.

You should be trained in proper oxygen system used and administration. Be sure to take an SDI CPROX course to learn all about this important first aid equipment and treatment, and how to use it properly.

Ladder

Whether you are diving from a large boat or a small boat, there must be some method for you to get back aboard the boat with all your dive gear. In most cases, the boat will be equipped with a ladder of some type that will make this possible.

The ladder must be of sufficient weight to carry two people. This is important in the event that you need to bring an unconscious diver back aboard the boat.

On very small boats, such as inflatables or fiberglass boats with low "freeboard," i.e., the distance from the deck to the water, it may be possible to boost yourself in over the side of the boat. To do this, you will probably need to remove your cylinder and weight belt.

First Aid Kit

Every boat should be equipped with at least a minimal first aid kit. You should be prepared to provide first aid to anyone on-board.

Cylinder Rack

Scuba cylinders can take up a lot of space on a small boat. A well-designed cylinder rack can help to reclaim this space so there is room for other equipment, as well as to dress in for diving. Cylinder racks also provide safer storage for scuba cylinders and help to prevent them from rolling around

Cylinder racks help free up deck space and increase safety aboard small boats.

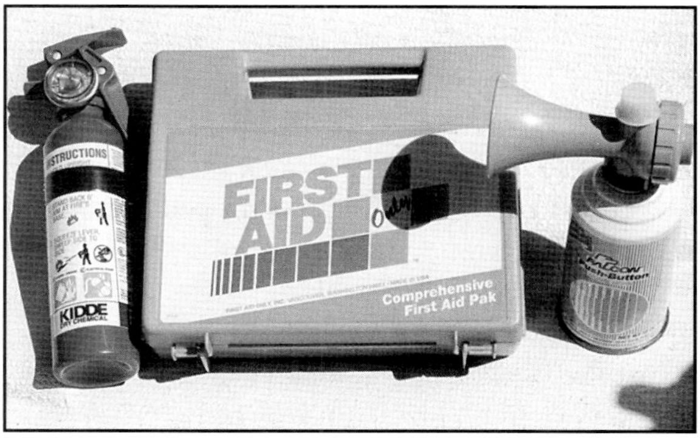

Every small boat should have a first aid kit, as well as an air horn and a fire extinguisher.

on the deck, which can damage the cylinder itself or other equipment, or result in an accident.

"Can't Do Without It!" Boat Gear

There are many items that are indispensable to boat operation, but amazingly enough, are not required by government regulations in most areas. Without question, you need to have the following items on board:

- An anchor and appropriate length of rope and chain
- Dock lines and fenders to secure the boat at the dock
- Spares and tools for minor repairs
- A compass and nautical charts
- Flashlight

Hard copy nautical charts are a must aboard a small boat, even if you have electronic navigation equipment.

Small boats should also be equipped with some type of device that will allow you to bail water out of the boat. Of course, there are many other accessories that can make boat diving both safer and more fun.

Required Gear for Boats

Certain pieces of equipment are required by the national maritime authorities or state agencies for boats between 16 (5 metres) and 65 feet (20 metres) in length. These items include the following:

- Fire Extinguisher
- Personal flotation devices (wearable lifejackets)
- Visual distress signaling devices
- Throwable flotation device
- Sound signaling device

In the U.S., visual signaling devices are required aboard small boats 16 feet (5 metres) in length or longer.

Personal Gear for Boat Diving

There are two categories of personal equipment that will help to improve your boat diving experience. Dry storage bags and boxes will help to protect your clothes and specialized gear like cameras during your trip. Hang-off lines are short lengths of line that can be rigged with a brass clip to support your equipment while entering or exiting the water. Signaling devices will help to ensure your safety in the event that you aren't able to make it back to the boat after you surface from a dive.

Dry Storage Bags and Boxes

When you go boat diving its inevitable that almost everything you take aboard the boat is going to get wet at one time or another during your trip. To protect your sensitive gear and other personal effects, you'll want to have a selection of dry bags and boxes. This is especially important if you do any diving from a small boat.

Dry bags are especially useful for transporting items like dry suits and dry suit underwear. If the inside of your dry suit gets wet during your trip your diving will be less than pleasant.

Dry boxes are made from heavy-duty plastics and have special padding inside them to protect delicate equipment like underwater cameras. These cases are designed with o-ring seals to help prevent water from entering the case, even if the box is submerged. Most underwater photographers use some type of dry box for transporting their camera or video systems.

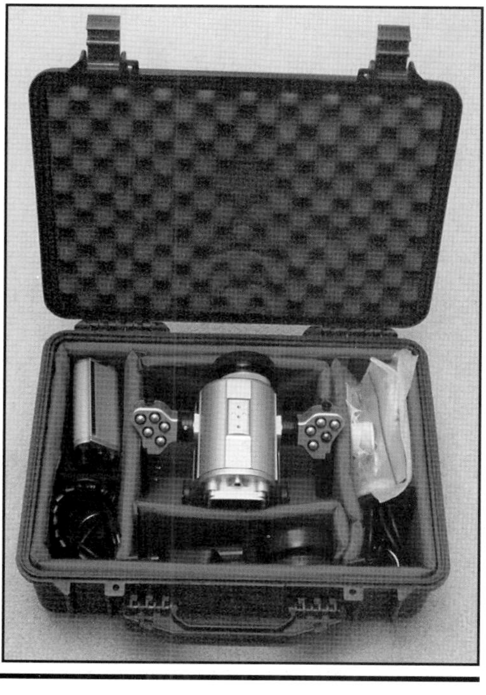

Waterproof cases are ideal for protecting equipment like camera systems.

Hang-Off Lines

A hang-off line is a specially rigged line designed to support any items of gear you don't want to wear or carry while entering or exiting the water from a boat. The line can be either polypropylene or nylon, rigged with an "eye" on one end and a brass clip on the other.

The eye of the hang-off line is attached to a cleat on the boat, and the clip is attached to the equipment you want to hang over the side. If you're diving from a small boat, hang-off lines are essential for handling your camera, goody bag, speargun, or other items. If you're diving from an inflatable, you'll almost certainly need a hang-off line to support your cylinder while you boost yourself back in over the side at the end of your dive.

If you do use hang-off lines its essential to remember to pull in any gear that's hanging over the side before the boat departs the dive site. If this is not done it's likely you'll either damage your gear or end up with a line in the propeller of the boat.

Be sure to attach some lines to your boat for hanging your gear in the water.

Surface Signaling Devices

Even if you are a careful and conscientious diver, at some point in your diving experience you may surface and find the dive boat on the distant horizon. This can happen if you are swept away by a current, or if sea conditions get rough and the boat's anchor line is broken. In these situations, there is no substitute for having a selection of signaling devices with you in the water.

Visual signaling devices include mirrors (made of stainless steel, not glass), "safety sausages" (inflatable tubes that stick high out of the water), and special waterproof flares. All of these items are small enough to fit in the pocket of a BC. Mirrors and safety sausages are effective primarily during daylight hours, but flares can be seen both during the day and at night. Visual devices can be effective at distances up to a mile or more, depending on weather conditions and time of day.

Audible signaling devices include whistles and air powered horns. There are several models of air-powered horns that are designed to connect between the low-pressure inflator hose from your cylinder and your BC's power inflator. While whistles are effective over short distances only, air powered horns are effective at distances of up to a mile (1.6 kilometres) or more depending on weather conditions.

Electronic signaling devices known as "EPIRBs" are also available. The word "EPIRB" is an abbreviation for Emergency Position Indicating Radio Beacon. The EPIRB puts out an electronic signal that allows the dive boat that is equipped with an EPIRB receiver to locate a diver who is on the surface, if the EPIRB is activated. These devices commonly send a signal that can be received by emergency services to help aid their location.

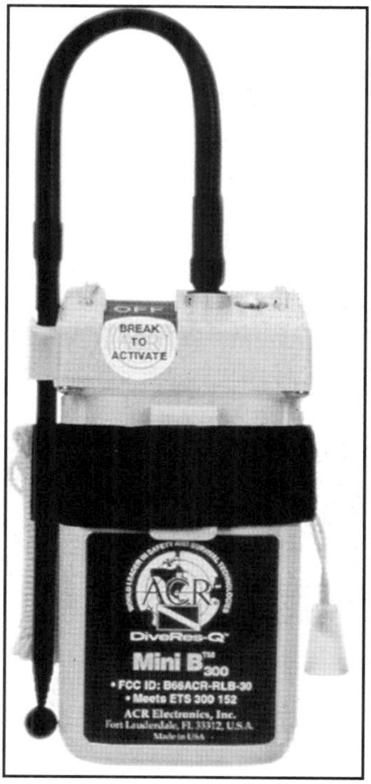

Devices like this Mini-EPIRB can save your life by helping to find you if you are lost at sea. (Photo courtesy ACR Marine Electronics.)

Marking Your Gear

For boat diving, you'll want to be sure that all of your gear is well marked to avoid having it confused with gear that belongs to other divers. Light colored gear can be marked with a waterproof marker. Darker gear may require the use of a rubber-based waterproof paint or marking stick.

Advance Planning for Boat Diving

Planning for a boat diving trip should take place well in advance of the trip itself so you have the time to ensure that your preparations are made properly and without haste. Your gear should be checked over several days prior to the trip to make sure that everything is in working order.

If you will be diving from a small boat that is owned by you or a friend, the boat should be checked over, too, to be sure it's properly prepared. Any repairs that need to be made should be taken care of well in advance of the trip. Your level of involvement in planning for the trip will depend on whether you are the boat operator of a small boat, or a passenger on whatever size boat the trip will be on.

If you'll be diving from a small boat it's also crucial to check the marine weather to monitor conditions for the area you want to dive. You can listen to the marine weather on a VHF radio, a marine weather radio, or read reports on internet websites.

Since weather forecasts can be wrong, it helps to develop local knowledge about weather conditions and consult a variety of sources when you are trying to decide whether conditions will be good for a particular trip. Internet sites that can be helpful in interpreting the weather are NOAA (National Oceanographic and Atmospheric Administration) weather buoys, Navy wave predictions for coastal areas, and "live" surf cameras for beach areas close to where you plan to dive.

Be sure to remember to pack any personal items that you may need for the boat. This list includes, but is not limited to:

- lunch
- sunglasses
- sunscreen
- money for cylinder fills
- hat
- towel(s)
- C-card and logbook
- topside camera & film

The boat operator will usually inform you if there are any special items that you need to bring. If you are traveling out of the country for a trip on a liveaboard boat, the operator will normally provide bedding, towels, all meals, and similar items. On domestic dive boats, however, if the trip is a

Many domestic boat trips depart at night or in the early morning hours.

multi-day excursion, you will probably need to bring your own bedding and towels.

Some boats include air fills in their daily price, while others will require you to pay for each fill. Not all boats have the capability to pump nitrox. Some domestic boats provide cylinders and weights, while others will require you to bring your own or rent them on board.

Be sure to arrive early enough to board the boat and stow all of your gear properly. Sometimes it's a long hike from the parking lot to the dock and if you have lots of gear, it may take you more than one trip to get everything on board. Charter dive boats will not wait for late passengers, unless you're traveling with a group that has chartered the whole boat and the group is delayed. If you miss the boat, you'll forfeit the price of your trip.

Preparing for Departure on a Charter Dive Boat

Once you've boarded the boat and you have all of your gear with you, check with the crew to see where they want you to stow your equipment. Your personal effects and things must be kept dry will normally be stowed in the cabin or on your bunk. Your dive gear will usually be assigned a space on deck. Most dive boats will not allow you to take any dive gear into the living accommodations (with the possible exception of an underwater camera).

Be sure to sign in on the boat's roster. The crew will usually want to see your proof of certification and/or your dive log. You will be asked to sign a waiver for your participation in diving activities. Bunks may be previously assigned, or may be available on a first-come, first-served basis, but ask before you take a bunk for yourself.

Be sure to listen carefully to any pre-departure briefing given by the divemaster or crew members. They will explain the location of the "heads" (bathrooms) and their operation, lifejacket use, meal times, and other important safety and procedural information. Most boats have their own specific procedure for requesting and getting your cylinder filled, so be sure you understand how it's done on any new boat from which you dive.

Preparing for Departure on a Private Dive Boat

Small boats are sometimes kept in slips in the water, but in most cases, private boats are usually kept on a trailer. The owner of the boat will tell you whether he needs help in hooking the boat to the trailer and where he wants you to meet him.

It's usually easiest to load gear aboard a small boat before it is launched,

Diving from a small boat requires different preparation and procedures than diving from a larger charter vessel.

but each skipper will have his own procedures. You may need to assist with handling dock lines and in fending the boat off from the dock. If you don't know how to properly fasten the lines to the dock, be sure to ask the owner of the boat. If the lines are fastened improperly, the boat could float away from the dock.

Risks in Boat Diving

Like all diving, there are some risks to boat diving that you should understand. These risks include being lost on the surface, being hit by a boat, or having the boat sink during a trip. These risks can usually be minimized through careful planning.

Although it's rare, divers are occasionally swept away by strong currents. Even more rare are situations where the boat crew leaves behind divers at a dive site. In either of these situations, there are no substitutes for effective visual, audible, and electronic signaling devices.

Each year, a certain number of divers, and swimmers, are hit by boats in the water. Although this could happen at any dive site, it's more likely at locations where there is heavy boat traffic.

These types of accidents are usually serious and can be fatal. You can minimize the risk of this type of accident by always diving from a boat that flies a dive flag and by taking care to surface as close to your boat as possible and avoiding long surface swims. This is especially important in areas where there is heavy boat traffic.

Probably the most unusual situation you might encounter while boat diving would be to have the dive boat sink during the course of a trip. Just as any car can be involved in an automobile accident, there is always the risk that any boat can sink. If you're booking a trip on a liveaboard boat be sure to select a dive operator with a good reputation. If you're diving from a private boat with someone whom you haven't been out with before, be sure to look over the boat carefully before leaving the dock to be sure that all of the necessary safety equipment is on board. Ask the owner about the operation of the boat so that you understand how to help if something goes wrong during the trip.

Always be sure to know where the lifejackets are stowed aboard the boat. If your boat is sinking in cold water, be sure to don your dive suit, if there's time to do so. For most divers, hypothermia is usually a greater risk than drowning when a boat sinks.

Scuba I.Q. Review

Boat diving provides the opportunity to travel to remote dive sites and have new experiences. Discuss the preparations for boat diving with your instructor so that you know what to expect when you board a dive boat for the first time.

1) Describe the flag that is used to signify sport diving operations.

2) Describe the alpha flag.

3) Explain how a current line is used.

4) Describe a drift diving line and float.

5) List two reasons why a VHF radio is preferred over a cell phone for communicating with shore in an emergency.

6) List four items that should be aboard any boat.

7) List four items that are required by the U.S. Coast Guard for all boats over 16 feet (5 metres) in length in U.S. waters.

8) List three types of devices used by divers for signaling on the surface of the water.

9) List two different sources of marine weather information for boat operators.

10) List three risks involved in boat diving.

Notes:

TRUK AGGRESSOR II

Chapter 3 Diving from Different Types of Boats

There are many different types of dive boats, and although the basic procedures for diving from most of them are pretty much the same, there are some adjustments that may need to be made in your procedures as you switch from boat to boat. Diving from a 17-foot (5 metre) long inflatable is not the same as diving from a 130-foot (40 metre) luxury charter boat. Whether you dive from a large boat or a small boat, safety should always be your foremost consideration.

In this chapter we'll examine techniques that you can use on any dive boat, as well as techniques that are specific to small boats and larger vessels.

Techniques Common to All Dive Boats

Entering the Water

One of the most important safety precautions you should observe when diving from any type of boat is to never enter the water until the captain has given the signal that it's okay to do so. The engines should be completely stopped and the anchor will usually be down before the captain will give the "all clear" sign.

The only exception to this rule would be if the boat is "live-boating," where the divers are dropped off at an offshore pinnacle surrounded by water too deep to anchor. In this type of operation, the boat moves over the pinnacle, cuts its engine, and the divers swim away from the boat and descend. The boat motors off away from the pinnacle and waits for the divers to surface before moving in to pick them up again when they are finished diving.

Once you have entered the water and moved clear of the entry area, be sure to stop and turn around to watch your partner enter the water. It's not uncommon for fins to come off or mask straps to be dislodged, especially if you are making an entry from a height. If your buddy has a fin come off, you'll

The giant stride is the preferred entry for use on large dive boats.

be in a much better position to retrieve it than they will be to retrieve their fins.

Swimming on the Surface

Be sure to avoid "skimming," i.e., swimming just below the surface of the water while on scuba. This is a good way to get hit by another boat, especially if you are in an area with heavy boat traffic. It is very difficult for a boat operator to see you if you are submerged just below the surface. You should be either snorkeling or swimming on your back on the surface, or fully submerged to a depth of at least 10 feet (3 metres) if on scuba.

If there is a strong current, the boat crew may rig a line from the stern of the boat to the anchor line. This "tag line" will allow you to pull yourself forward to the anchor line where you can make your descent ahead of the boat.

Always Start Your Dive Into the Current

Be sure to always start your dive into the current, unless you're participating in a drift dive. At the end of your dive you'll be able to return to the boat easily with the current.

Be Back on Board When Requested

If the divemaster or captain asks you to be back on board at a particular time, be sure to make every effort to follow their request. If you're not on board when requested, you may hold up the entire boat. If you get the captain angry enough, you may be told not to come out on the boat in the future.

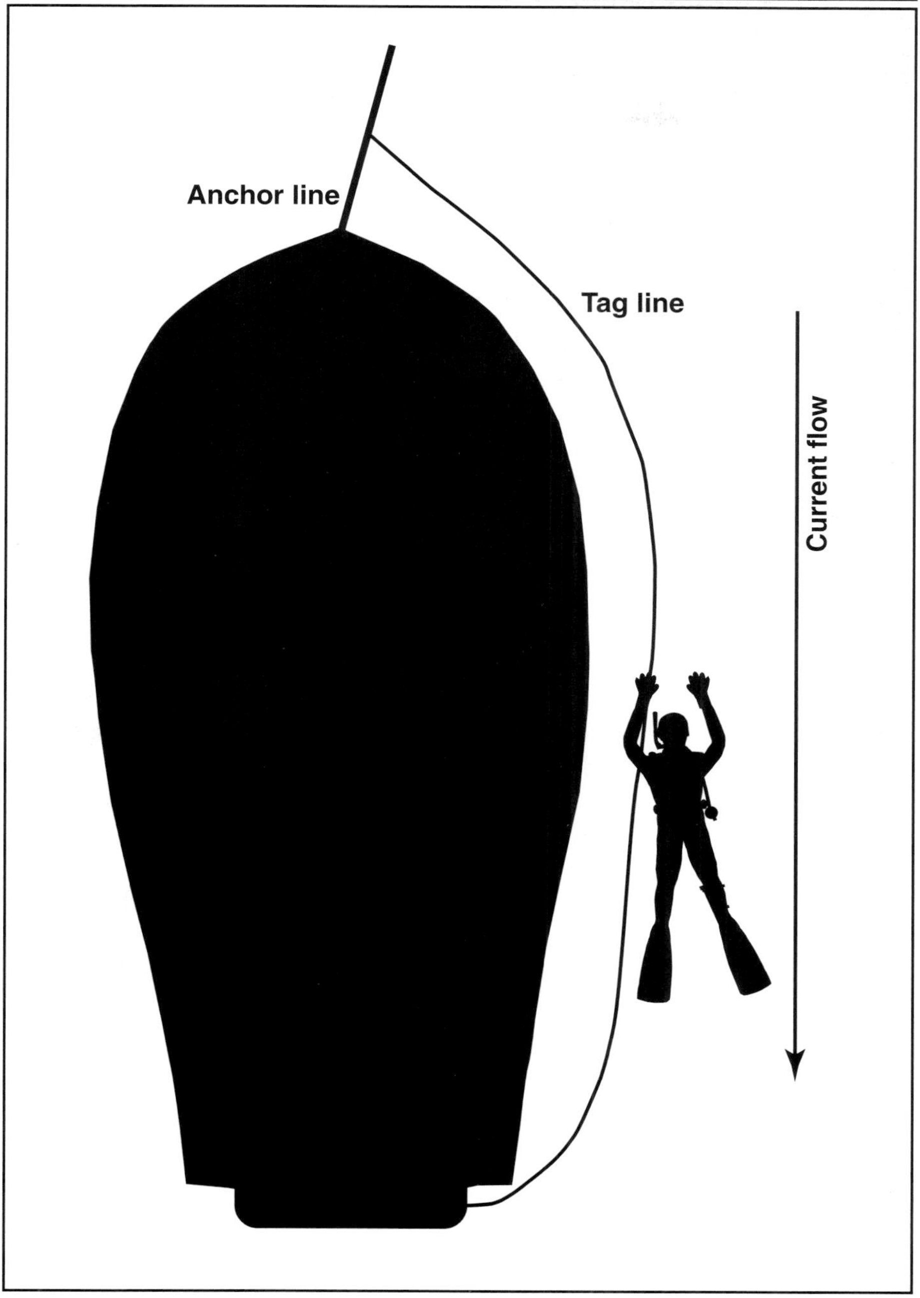

If there is a strong current, a tag line can be used to allow divers to pull themselves from the rear of the boat to the anchor line to make their descent.

Be Sure to Heed Any Diver Recall

Many dive boats today are equipped with a diver recall device that is used to signal all the divers in the water that they need to return to the boat in the event of an emergency. When activated, the device sounds similar to a siren. If you are underwater and hear a sound like this, surface as soon as possible and return to the boat.

Signalling on the Surface

If the boat crew gives you the okay sign at a distance, either hands clasped overhead or one hand on top of the head, be sure to respond back so that they know that you are "okay." If you are trying to signal to them and can't get their attention, don't hesitate to use your air horn or whistle.

Whatever signal you use, be sure to make it large or loud enough and wait for a response from the boat before you stop signalling.

Use the Current Line if You Need It!

If you find yourself behind the boat and there's a strong current running, don't be embarrassed to use the current line if you need it. It's better to use the line than to force the boat crew to perform a rescue or launch a skiff to pick you up.

Clear the Swimstep or Ladder Quickly

While you are waiting your turn to exit the water and board the boat, be sure to stay out from under other divers. If they fall backwards while wearing a scuba cylinder you could be seriously injured if you are hit.

When you are returning to the boat, be sure to board it quickly and move out of the way so that other divers can get on board swiftly. This is especially important if sea conditions are rough.

Be sure to stay out from underneath the boat's ladder underwater to avoid injury.

Stow Your Gear Between Dives

Whether you're on a large boat or a small boat, everyone will appreciate it if you properly stow your gear in your assigned space (or dive bag) between dives. This will help to keep the deck clear and your equipment is less likely to be lost or damaged. Of course, all of your personal gear should be marked for identification.

No Wet Gear Below Decks

No matter what type of boat you are on, large or small, most skippers will not allow you to take wet equipment (suits, BCs, etc.) into the bunk or cabin area. When wet gear is taken below it dampens the carpet and makes the bunk areas moldy and musty. Some boats prohibit towels that have been used to dry off your body after diving from being taken into the accomodations.

If you want to stay with good terms with the captain and crew, follow their instructions and only put your gear where it's supposed to go.

Take Care with Weights and Cylinders

Cylinders and weight belts can do a lot of damage to a boat if they are carelessly handled. While some boats may allow you to enter the dining area (the "mess") while you are wet, weight belts and cylinders are usually forbidden. Be sure to carefully stow and secure your cylinder and weight belt whenever you are not actually wearing them and don't wear them inside the cabin.

Diving from Small Private Boats

A small boat might be best defined as any boat that will fit onto a trailer. While regulations vary from state to state, by this definition, the largest boat that would be considered a "small boat" is about 28 feet (8.5 metres) in

Most small dive boats are kept on trailers and must be launched at the start of the diving day.This is a "RHIB," rigid hull inflatable boat.

length. Most small boats are trailered rather than kept in a slip in a marina.

Some large dive boats also carry smaller boats aboard them that may be used to pick up divers who are caught in a current behind the boat, transport divers across shallow reefs where the large boat can't maneuver, or to take divers into shore. These smaller boats are usually either inflatables or small fiberglass skiffs. You may hear these boats referred to as "tenders."

There are several different popular types of small boats including inflatables, aluminum boats, and fiberglass boats. Each type of boat has advantages and disadvantages for diving.

Inflatable Boats

Probably the most popular and economical type of small boat used for diving is the inflatable. Inflatables are great boats for diving because they can be easily transported and they are very forgiving when they bump into a dock or gear knocks into the sides of the pontoons. They are so light-weight that even a 17-foot (5 metres) inflatable can be trailered by most passenger cars.

The biggest disadvantage to inflatables is that they have very limited deck space. There just isn't much room for your gear when you are diving from an inflatable. They are also very "wet" boats, i.e., everything inside the boat may get wet, especially when conditions are rough.

One type of inflatable that is very popular for diving is known as a rigid hull inflatable, "RHIB,"or "RIB." These boats feature a fiberglass keel with inflatable pontoons for the sides of the boat. RIBs are very fast and are especially popular with divers in Europe.

Inflatable boats are excellent coastal boats, but unless you are diving from a RIB, you probably won't be venturing more than a few miles from shore. Larger RIBs can be easily outfitted with lights and electronics for navigation. This type of boat is especially popular in the U.K. and Europe.

Aluminum and Fiberglass Boats

Aluminum and fiberglass boats tend to be larger, heavier boats and when they are on a trailer, they require a heavy-duty tow vehicle to transport them for launching. These types of boats tend to be more expensive to purchase and operate than inflatable boats.

The advantages to these types of boats for diving is that they typically have more deck space than an inflatable boat of comparable size. They also tend to handle better in rougher seas due to their greater weight. Fiberglass and aluminum boats are often equipped with enclosed cabins that allow you to get out of the weather to change clothes and/or load and unload cameras.

Small Boat Charters

In many parts of the U.S. small boats carrying up to six passengers are available for dive charters. On these types of operations, the captain may function both as the skipper and divemaster. These types of operations are typically referred to as "six-pack charters."

Most six pack charters do not feature all of the comforts that larger boats offer, but in many cases they travel much faster than larger boats and can maneuver in shallower waters. This makes them ideal for single day dive trips. However, some boats of this size may not be equipped with a shower or a "head" (marine toilet).

The typical six pack operation will feature a boat less than 30 feet (9 metres) in length and the boat will not usually be equipped with a compressor. You may need to supply extra cylinders if you want to make more than one dive, or the boat may provide them. One of the biggest advantages to a six-pack is that once you are on the site, there will be fewer divers in the water.

Pre-Departure Procedures

Prior to diving, you must load your gear on the boat. Since equipment on a small boat tends to get wet, it's critical to pack your gear the right way to ensure a good trip.

If you're diving from an inflatable, you may find that the best way to load

Most small boats do not have a toilet, known as a "head" in nautical terms. You'll want to try to anticipate your needs in this area before the boat departs the dock.

your gear is to assemble your cylinder, BC, and regulator and put them in the boat this way, rather than taking them aboard as separate components. For boats less than 15 feet (3 metres) in length, especially inflatables, it's much easier to put your diving suit on at the dock than to suit up on the boat. If you're wearing a suit like a two-piece farmer john (long-john), it's a good idea to put at least the pants on before leaving the dock.

If you decide to dress in before you board the boat, you may want to leave your clothes in the car rather than taking them aboard the boat. This is also a good idea if the boat tends to be "wet," taking spray over the side as you travel to the dive site. If you set up your cylinder and don your wetsuit, you can carry your mask, fins, snorkel, and gloves in a compact mesh goody bag that won't take up much room aboard the boat.

Waterproof bags and boxes are invaluable items for protecting anything you want to keep dry while you're diving from a small boat. Cylinder racks like Pelican® racks are ideal for keeping multiple cylinders organized and out of the way. Just be sure the cylinder rack is fastened to the deck in some way that it won't go skidding across the deck if seas get rough.

Small Boat Skills

Once you're at the dive site and the boat is anchored securely, it's time to get ready to dive. Before you do anything else, don't forget to put your dive flag up so that it can be seen. This is the time to put your current line out and your ladder over the side, too.

Although it may not always be possible, ideally there should be someone aboard the boat who knows how to operate it, whenever divers are in the water. If you surface down current during a running tide, or if the boat drags anchor while you are underwater, there is no substitute for having someone aboard who knows how to handle the situation.

On some small boats, particularly smaller inflatables, it may not be possible to stand up to get dressed in. Stay low when moving about on a boat with poor stability.

For most dive operations you'll find it's convenient to have some lines with brass snap hooks on the end of them that you can use to hang equipment or other items off the back of the boat. For example, you may want to hang your camera over the side at the start or the end of your dive, or your goody bag holding any game you have collected during your dive. Some divers find it's easier to put their cylinder on in the water and fasten their cylinder to a hang-off line so it doesn't float away while they're getting in the water.

The best way to hang your cylinder over the side is to wrap the line

Getting dressed aboard a small dive boat can be awkward, especially if the seas are rough.

around the neck of the cylinder twice and fasten the clip back on the "live" end on the line. Be sure to turn the air on to your regulator before you hang your cylinder over the side, otherwise, you'll flood the first stage. Put just enough air in the BC so that the cylinder floats. If the BC is too full, it will be difficult to slide into your cylinder harness in the water.

There are several ways to enter the water from a small boat, including the use of the backwards roll and the giant stride. If you're diving from a boat like an inflatable, where the sides of the boat are low to the water, the best entry to use is the backwards roll. Be sure to hold your mask tightly to your face as you flip over the side of the boat. Wait until you stop spinning before you start swimming to avoid hitting your head on the side of the boat.

If you're diving from an inflatable and prefer to put your cylinder on in the water, you can just sit on one of the pontoons, facing the water, and simply slide down the side of the pontoon. Have your dive partner hold your cylinder upright in a vertical position so you can slide into your BC easily.

Once you and your buddy are ready to go, swim down the anchor line to check the position of the anchor on the bottom. You want to make sure that is in an area where it will not hang up on rocks, wreckage, or other obstructions when it is time to pull it up. If the anchor is not where you want it, don't hesitate to pick it up and move it.

You also want to be sure that the anchor has a good "bite" in the bottom and that the anchor line will not be chafing on any obstructions. Take a fix on the anchor so you'll be able to relocate it at the end of your dive if you want to make your ascent on the anchor line.

After you have made your dive and you're ready to board the boat, you'll probably want to remove your cylinder and hang it off prior to climbing back aboard. This isn't necessary on boats that have sturdy ladders, but if you're diving from an inflatable, it's almost impossible to get back aboard if you are

If you're diving from a small boat, it's wise to check the anchor at the start of your dive.

It's usually necessary to remove your tank to climb back aboard a small inflatable.

still wearing your cylinder. You'll want to remove your weight belt, too, particularly if the boat is not equipped with a ladder and you need to boost yourself in over the side.

It's a good habit to recover any gear that you've got hanging over the side as soon as you get back aboard. Divers who forgot to recover items left hanging over the side have destroyed countless pieces of gear when they motored away from the dive site. Prior to heading home at the end of the day, be sure that your gear is properly stowed so it won't go flying around the boat or over the side.

Before you pull anchor, take one last check around to be sure that you've pulled the ladder up, all lines are in from over the side, and the diver's flag is taken down.

Recovering an Unconscious Diver

One often overlooked skill for divers who use small boats are techniques for recovering an injured or unconscious diver back aboard the boat. This can be a difficult or impossible task if you are alone and have no training in how to do this.

One method for recovering an unconscious diver is to remove their cylinder and weight belt, and yours, then place the diver on one of your thighs, facing you. Place their arms around your neck, as though they were embracing you. You can then climb the ladder, a rung at a time.

Diving from Large Charter Vessels

Dive charter vessels vary widely in different locations in their accommodations and services. Even in the same area, each boat may be very different in terms of what they provide for the diver.

On the east coast of the U.S., most charter boats do not have an air compressor on board for filling cylinders, so each diver must bring additional cylinders if they want to make more than one dive a day. The boats tend to be not as luxurious as some of the liveaboard boats that operate in the tropics.

On the west coast of the U.S., most boats are equipped for overnight trips because the offshore islands provide good anchorages at remote distances from the coast. These boats are equipped with compressors, hot showers, and bunks, and are set up to provide meals for all of the divers on board.

Some of the most luxurious dive boats to be found are located at internationally famous dive destinations around the world. Most of these vessels are set up to provide extremely comfortable accommodations combined with services that make your diving almost effortless. Many have the capability to process film on-board and edit underwater video.

The Channel Islands off California are popular diving destinations for multi-day dive trips.

These types of boats are usually completely self-sufficient and are able to travel to the most remote dive locations. Depending on the number of passengers, they can normally carry enough provisions for at least a week of operations at a remote site.

Large Vessel Dive Operations

Some of the precautions and techniques that you should follow when operating from a large charter vessel are a bit unique. For example, if you change the film in your camera at the end of the day, you'll want to be sure to stow your photo gear in a secure location where it can't fall if the boat moves during the night. Although most dive boats today have specific camera storage tables, not all do, and divers have had their equipment damaged when it's fallen off a table as the boat motored in heavy seas.

Depending on the design of the boat you may find yourself entering from the bow, the side, or the stern of the boat. Some boats on the west coast of the U.S. use a bow door, when there is a strong current, to eliminate the need to pull yourself up to the anchor line using a tag line from the stern. You jump in at the bow and immediately grab the anchor line to pull yourself down to the bottom. There's no disadvantage to this type of entry although it may be a long drop to the water due to the height of the bow! If the distance from the deck to the water is great, bring your legs together rather than keeping

Some boats are equipped with bow doors to allow you to enter the water at the front of the vessel.

spread when you do your giant stride entry.

Many boats use a side entry "gate" or "door." Although the height is greater than a stern entry, it is still not the height of the bow and puts you that much closer to the anchor line for your descent.

Many boats that operate in the tropics use a dive platform located on the stern for both entry to and exit from the water. This is the lowest "impact" point of entry on most boats.

Be sure to only move yourself and your equipment to the entry area when you are actually ready to enter the water. You don't want to block other divers who are entering or exiting the water if you're not truly prepared to move.

Be sure to identify your cylinder when it needs to be filled so that you don't miss a dive or hold up your dive partner when it's time to enter the water.

Boat Diving Emergencies

Two situations that directly relate to boat diving are finding yourself behind the boat in a strong current and responding to an underwater recall. While neither of these situations should be life threatening, they both deserve special mention.

In most cases where you surface behind the boat in a current, you should be able to pull yourself back to the boat on the current line. If you miss the line, do not attempt to swim against the current, as you will only exhaust yourself. Instead, inflate your buoyancy compensator to give yourself positive buoyancy and attempt to signal the boat using your surface signaling devices.

Your initial attempt to signal the boat should be made using either a whistle or an air horn. If this doesn't work, use visual signals, such as a flare or inflatable signaling device ("safety sausage"). If you are unable to signal the boat, you should attempt to swim to land, if you are close enough to do so. If you are out of sight of land, your only alternative would be to ditch your weights and await rescue.

In the event that you are underwater and hear a recall signal from the boat, you should begin a normal ascent immediately. You will not be able to make a safety stop, however, and you should proceed directly to the surface, while listening for the boat's engines and watching for signs of boat movement. If you hear the boat's engines or see the boat is underway, you must be extremely cautious not to surface near the boat.

Scuba I.Q. Review

Before your first boat dive, discuss the procedures you'll be following with your instructor. See if you can answer the following questions and check your understanding by reviewing your answers with your instructor.

1) Explain why it is important to wait for the captain or crew to signal that it's safe to enter the water before leaving the boat.

2) Define the term "skimming" and explain why this is a dangerous practice.

3) Explain what a "diver recall device" is and the procedures you should follow if you hear one while you are underwater.

4) What type of entry is most commonly used when diving from an inflatable boat?

5) List 3 water entry points commonly used when diving from large vessels.

Chapter 4
Drift Diving

Drift diving is like effortless underwater flying. When you are neutrally buoyant and soaring along with a gentle current in clear water you get a perspective on the underwater world that is difficult to capture in any other way.

Depending on where you dive, different divemasters and diving operations may employ different techniques for drift diving. However, in general, the divemaster will almost always be in the water with you and he will control the direction and course of the dive, the depth, and the length of the dive.

In almost all drift diving operations the dive boat will follow the group so that they can pick up the divers as they surface. Drift diving requires a skilled boat operator to conduct operations properly.

As previously mentioned, you should be proficient in your diving skills to participate in drift diving. On a drift dive it is usually not possible to stop to deal with an equipment problem or other difficulty, although you may be able to get behind a current or wreck that will block the current. You must be capable of performing a hovering safety stop and maintaining a constant depth to participate in drift diving. The faster the current, the more skilled you should be as a diver to comfortably participate in a given drift dive.

Drift Diving Techniques

Some dive masters use a buoy and a line to control a drift dive. The initial descent is made with the divemaster as he pays out the line as the group heads for the bottom. The buoy provides a reference point on the surface for the location of the group and is helpful to the boat captain in the event that waves on the surface make it difficult for the skipper to see the divers' bubbles. Each individual diver must be equipped with both a sound signaling

It's important for for everyone in the group to make their descent at the start of a drift dive at the same time.

device and a visual signaling device.

If you have difficulty equalizing your ears during the descent, be sure to maintain contact with the buoy line. If you lose contact with the line or the group, you should ascend immediately but cautiously, keeping a close eye out for boat traffic.

When you are making a drift dive, it is essential for you and your dive partner to stay within sight of the divemaster at all times during the dive. Do not wander off from the group. Depending on the visibility and other factors, some divemasters may require novice drift divers to maintain physical contact with the buoy line.

Never try to fight the current during a drift dive. This will only wear you out and cause you to consume your air faster. Relax and let the current propel you through the water.

If you hug the seabed it is possible to kick up silt with your fins. It quickly overtakes and envelopes you in the current. A simple technique to avoid this is to swim at an angle to the current such as 10-20 degrees to the right. You will always have clean water surging past you if you stop to look at an item of interest.

Whenever you are drift diving, you should keep an eye on what features of the underwater terrain are in front of you. If you see that the current is going to push you into some type of hazard, such as a fishing net, start maneuvering to one side or the other of the hazard well before you reach it. If you wait until you are on top of the hazard it will become difficult to avoid it.

If you consume air faster than the rest of the divers in the group, the divemaster will usually send you and your dive partner up to complete your safety stop. If the divemaster is using a line and float, stay close to the line and float while completing your stop. If the divemaster is not using a line and float, be sure to stay above the group and keep them in sight as you hover at 10-15 feet (3-5 metres).

If you consume air slower than the rest of the group, be sure to ascend when the divemaster gives you the signal to do so, even if you still have plenty of air remaining in your cylinder. Continuing on a drift dive without the group can be very hazardous to your safety.

When you complete your safety stop, cautiously surface, keeping a sharp eye for any boats that may be approaching. If the dive goes as it should, the boat should be very close to you and prepared to pick you up. Don't try to swim to the boat – the boat will normally come to you.

As the boat approaches, do not swim to it until the boat is stopped in the water and either the deckhand or captain gives you the signal that it is safe to approach the boat, Once you are given the signal to approach, swim quickly to the boat and climb aboard.

Drift Diving Emergencies

The most serious emergency that might occur specific to drift diving would be to find yourself separated from the group. In most cases, if you find yourself separated from the group, cautiously surface while keeping an eye out for boats, inflate your BC, and signal to get the attention of the boat crew to pick you up.

Everyone must stay within sight of the divemaster during a drift dive.

Down draft currents exist in some parts of the world that can force a diver into deeper water than planned. If this type of current encountered, it is essential that you overcome the current by using your buoyancy compensator, without rising too rapidly through the water column. If you can't create sufficient buoyancy using your BC you may need to ditch your weight belt to ascend.

Scuba I.Q. Review

Drift diving is an activity that requires good buoyancy control. You must be comfortable in your diving skills to participate in drift diving. Discuss the procedures your instructor will use to conduct your drift dive and review the following questions.

1) Define the term "drift diving."

2) Explain what equipment a divemaster will normally use to control a drift dive.

3) Explain the procedure you should follow if you become separated from the rest of the group that you are diving with during a drift dive.

Chapter 5 Researching Shipwrecks

One of the most exciting aspects of wreck diving is discovering a "new" wreck, i.e., one that has never been explored by other divers. Part of the thrill of this type of find is that a previously unexplored wreck is usually undisturbed and more likely to be in the same condition it was on the day it sank.

Finding new shipwrecks requires research to uncover the history surrounding the sinking of any vessel. Fortunately, it's easier today than ever to do research.

Wreck diving is more meaningful when you know the history of the wreck and the circumstances that caused it to end up on the bottom. In this chapter, we'll explore the various sources of information regarding shipwrecks, the causes of shipwrecks, ownership of shipwrecks, and some of the laws governing shipwrecks.

Information Sources

There are many sources of information that you can use to do research on a particular wreck. These include dive guides, books, television specials, newspapers, the Internet, and eyewitness accounts. The more information you have, the better your chances of locating a particular wreck. Try to avoid depending on one source to locate a wreck.

Dive Guides

As strange as it may seem, not all divers are interested in shipwrecks. Occasionally, you may find a divemaster who will divulge the location of a little known shipwreck. This type of information makes wreck location easy.

Many books have been written about shipwrecks.

Books

There are numerous books that have been written about shipwrecks and many of them were not written for divers, but for people interested in nautical history. These types of books are often an excellent source of information, even though they may not help you to locate the wreck itself.

Pay attention to references to books that are out-of-print. If you are looking for an older wreck, out-of-print books often have information you may not locate anywhere else. With the use of the Internet, it is much easier to find books like these.

Television Specials

While it's unlikely that you would find useful information on an undiscovered wreck on television, it's not impossible. No information source should be overlooked.

Newspapers

Local newspapers are usually very good sources of information on shipwrecks in your area. Although the publishers of the newspapers will rarely give you access to their archives, many local libraries will maintain old copies of newspapers on microfilm that can be read with the library's microfilm reader. Most microfilm readers have copy machines connected to them so that you can print out any article that interests you.

Libraries

In addition to old newspapers, neighborhood libraries will commonly have books and pamphlets that have been written about local events with information that is not available elsewhere. Be sure to get to know the reference librarian, as they will frequently be able to direct you to sources for the information you need.

Historical Societies

Most cities of any size will have a community history society that collects and catalogs historical data that is of local interest. These organizations collect information and publications on a wide range of subjects. Their members are typically more than willing to share any information they have on regional history.

Shipwreck Survivors Association

Various associations in Europe support survivors of vessels that sank during a military conflict, especially where loss of life was a factor. These associations provide an encyclopedic insight into role and mission, layout and damage to the vessel, acts of courage or bravery during sinking, cargo and its placement and information regarding position at the time of sinking.

Many of these associations regard it courteous to inform them of the intentions of the diving party and offer both information and sponsorship support to a bona-fide group.

Local libraries usually have great information on regional maritime history.

Maritime museums are a focal point for every type of information on local nautical history.

Maritime Museums

Maritime museums are usually a collecting point for all manner of documents, photographs, artifacts, and other data pertaining to shipwrecks. Many maritime museums have their own research libraries and although they may not be open to the public, if you make a specific request for information you will generally receive assistance.

Shipyard Drawings

Sometimes its possible to obtain the original construction drawings of the ship. If you can obtain these they will help you greatly in understanding the layout of the wreck and the parts you are looking at on the bottom.

Local Fishermen

Recreational and commercial fishermen are often knowledgeable about local shipwreck locations. It's not uncommon for them to lose gear on these hulks and make a point of knowing where they are on the bottom. These are people who are well worth getting to know. Other than dive guides who have actually been on a wreck, fishermen are normally able to give wreck locations better than anyone else.

Commercial fishermen usually know the location of many shipwrecks. (© S. Barsky. All rights reserved.)

Eyewitness Accounts

Eyewitness accounts can be quite useful in piecing together the background information on a wreck. However, you must be cautious in accepting an eyewitness account as "fact," as these observations are often made during emotional moments.

Wreck locations based on eyewitness accounts may be inaccurate unless the wreck sank due to striking a known hazard or it was immediately adjacent to a recognized landmark. The visual perspective of a person viewing a sinking from a distance on shore may be distorted, leading you to search in the wrong place.

Wreck Site Drawings

The National Park Service's Submerged Cultural Resources Unit has mapped many of the wrecks that lie in national parks in the United States.

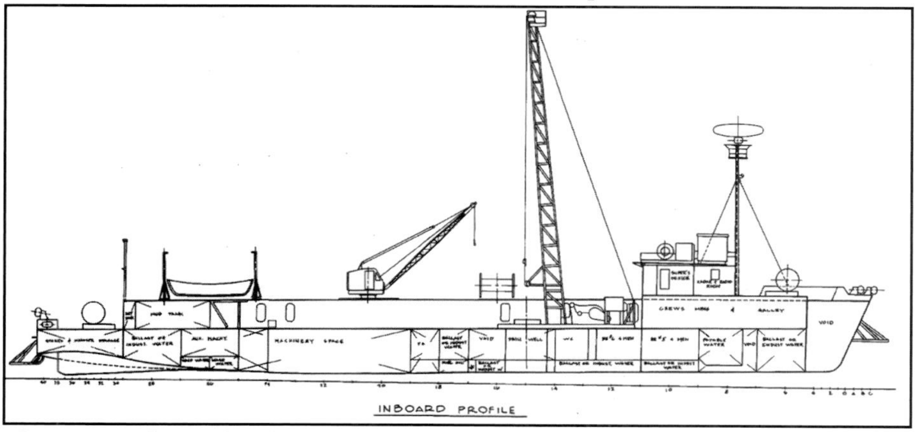

If you can obtain the drawings that were used to build the ship, you will better understand the parts of the wreck you see on the bottom. This is a drawing of the "SM-1" a drill ship that sank near Santa Barbara, California.

The drawings that they have produced of these wrecks provide divers with outstanding maps to help interpret the wrecks as they exist today. They have created drawings for many wrecks around the U.S. including several wrecks at Channel Islands National Park off Santa Barbara, Micronesia, and the *U.S.S. Arizona* in Pearl Harbor, Hawaii.

Why Ships Sink

Wrecks occur for many different reasons and the cause of the sinking will normally play a tremendous role in the condition of the wreck. Some of the causes of wrecks include failures in navigation, collisions with other ships, fires, warfare, and intentional sinking for insurance purposes.

The cause of the wreck may also play a role in planning your dive. For example, if the wreck occurred because the ship struck a rocky reef, you may need to anchor your boat at a good distance from the reef to avoid damage to your own boat.

Wrecks that went aground in shallow water may only be approachable under certain tidal conditions, i.e., only when the tide is high. Other wrecks may be in areas of heavy boat traffic, making diving operations hazardous. Frequently, the cause of the sinking can provide many clues that will help you pinpoint the location of the wreck.

Many of the wrecks in the world today are where they are due to military battles. Off the east coast of the U.S. and off Great Britain there are many

Ships become wrecks for many different reasons, including navigational errors, mechanical failures, and fires, to name a few causes.

This submarine, the Bluegill, was originally sunk intentionally by the U.S. Navy in 130 feet of water near Lahaina Harbor, in Hawaii. It was used by Navy divers for submarine rescue training. The wreck was extremely popular with sport divers, many of whom suffered decompression sickness diving the wreck. Unfortunately, the Navy ultimately moved the wreck out to deeper water.

ships that were sunk during World War II.

Many wrecks are sunk intentionally today to serve as artificial reefs for fishing and/or diving. These ships are normally stripped of all hazardous materials and holes are cut in them to make them more accessible for divers to explore them with reduced risks.

Not all Wrecks are Ships

While most people think of ships when they think of "wreck" diving, there are many other types of "wrecks" that divers enjoy exploring. For example, it is not uncommon in many locations to find airplanes that have crashed into the water, that have not been salvaged. In Chuuk, there are even tanks in shallow water and on the deck of transport vessels.

In some locations, divers and fishing groups have deliberately (with government permission) sunk a variety of other types of vehicles to serve as dive sites. Some other items that have been purposely placed on the bottom include automobiles, buses, airplanes, and trolleys. The remains of these objects can provide interesting dives and photographic subjects.

A tank sits on the deck of a ship in Chuuk. In other locations you may find planes, trolley cars, and other vehicles underwater.

Ships in Fresh Water

While there are probably more shipwrecks in salt water, there are also many excellent wrecks in fresh water, too. One of the best places to dive shipwrecks in the U.S. is at Isle Royale National Park on Lake Superior.

Fresh water shipwrecks are not subject to the same deterioration that occurs in salt water. There is almost no corrosion due to the lack of salt in the water and there are none of the marine worms that attack wooden hulls. Shipwrecks in fresh water are often nearly in the same condition as the day they sank.

Wreck History

In filling out your knowledge of the wrecks you dive, you'll want to know the answers to the following questions:

- When and where was the ship built?
- What is the history of ownership of the wreck?
- Was the wreck involved in any historical incidents, other than its own sinking?
- Who were the passengers on board the wreck when it went down?
- Was the wreck carrying any cargo? weapons?
- What were the circumstances of the sinking?
- Were any salvage attempts made on the wreck?
- Were any lives lost in the sinking of the wreck?

Who is the Current Owner of the Wreck?

The ownership of recent wrecks is usually easy to determine, but the ownership of older wrecks may be difficult to identify. In most cases, you are perfectly free to dive on and explore any shipwreck you happen to discover. However, there are shipwrecks that you may be forbidden to dive, due to the value of their cargo (which is being salvaged), their historical significance (archaeological value), or their designation as a war grave, i.e., because people died when the ship went down.

There are many shipwrecks that hold valuable cargo, or the ship itself may have value as "scrap" to a salvage company. Under these circumstances, the owners of the ship may not be the original owners, as the rights may have been acquired by a salvage firm.

Older wrecks that have archaeological or other historical significance may be under the jurisdiction of local or Federal government agencies, or may be under excavation by a university or other private research firm. There may be restrictions that prevent you from diving this type of wreck.

Wrecks that are designated as "war graves" are ships that hold the remains of military personnel who died on board. In some situations, you may be denied access to these types of wrecks.

In all cases, it is recommended that you do not remove artifacts (portholes, lamps, cargo, etc.) from shipwrecks for several reasons. When artifacts are removed from a wreck, it diminishes the wreck diving experience for other divers, especially if the wreck is damaged when the artifacts are taken. If the wreck is still owned by the original owners, or belongs to a salvage firm, any removal of items from the wreck is considered theft and you could be subject to criminal prosecution.

In the United States, depending on the age of the wreck, and/or its historical significance, most wrecks are protected by Federal law under a bill known as "The Abandoned Shipwreck Act," or more formally as Public Law 100-298. By this law, which went into effect in 1988, the states acquired jurisdiction over all shipwrecks up to three miles from shore. If you remove artifacts from a ship protected by this law you may be subject to Federal prosecution. In other countries, there are similar laws protecting wrecks from unauthorized salvage.

In the United Kingdom, all items from a wreck found on the seabed have an owner. The item must be declared to the "Receiver of Wreck", part of the Maritime & Coastguard Agency (MCA). The role of the Receiver is to find the owner and negotiate salvage rights or in many cases transfer of ownership to the finder. The dive vessel skipper will have paperwork for you to fill out and post.

The Receiver of Wreck also designates specific sites as licensed sites if viewed as a wreck of historic importance. Some shipwrecks, often-military owned war graves, are designated total exclusion sites to divers with fines up to £5000.00 ($7000.00) imposed on divers who ignore the designation set out in 2001.

Scuba I.Q. Review

Knowing the history of a wreck will give greater significance to each dive that you make on it. Discuss the historical aspects of the wrecks you will be diving during your training with your instructor as you review the following questions.

1) List five information sources that can help provide you with information about shipwrecks.

2) List four reasons why ships sink.

3) List two reasons why you may be denied access to dive on certain wrecks.

4) List two reasons why you should not remove artifacts from shipwrecks.

SCUBA DIVING INTERNATIONAL

Chapter 6 Risks of Wreck Diving

All diving has some level of risk, and wreck diving is no exception. However, wreck diving poses no more risks than most other types of recreational diving.

Risks that should be recognized in wreck diving include entanglement with nets and lines, cuts from sharp metal, problems with navigation, and the dangers associated with wreck penetration. In addition, due to the location of some wrecks, there could be dangers for your boat either from environmental hazards or due to heavy boat traffic.

Entanglement

Although you could become entangled in a fishing net or monofilament fishing line anywhere underwater, wrecks act as a "magnet" for both sport and commercial fishermen, just as they do for divers. The fish that congregate on a wreck attract fishermen who lose their nets, lines, and hooks. If you're not alert, you can become entangled in a fisherman's lost gear.

When they are present, a commercial fisherman's lost fishing net usually poses a greater risk for the diver than a sportsman's fishing line, simply because nets have more surface area and mass. If you accidentally swim into a net, or worse yet, back into a net, the net can become snagged on numerous pieces of your gear. Fortunately, a net that has been submerged for some period of time will probably have debris hung up in it, such as drift kelp, or algae growing on it, which will help to make it easier to see underwater.

Depending on lighting conditions, monofilament line may be almost invisible in the water, and although there may not be as much of it, it can still become wrapped around a cylinder valve or snagged under a cylinder band on your buoyancy compensator.

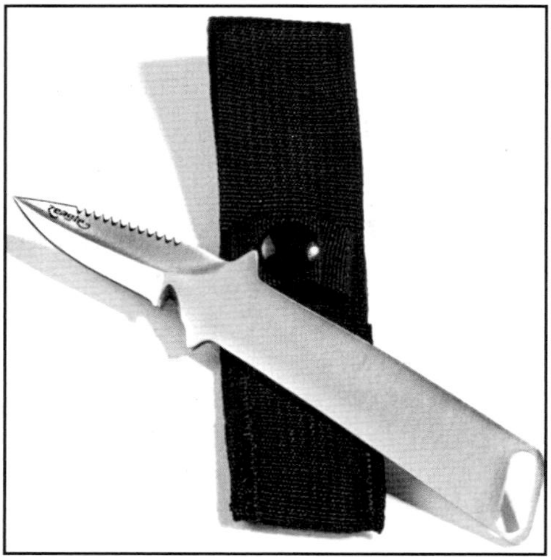

A sharp knife is an important accessory for wreck diving.(Photo courtesy Zeagle Systems, Inc.

If you do become entangled in a net or fishing line, the most important thing you can do is to stop swimming and slowly free yourself from the line. If you thrash and struggle there's a good chance you will only make your situation worse. It's most difficult to disengage yourself from a net or line that has caught on your cylinder valve or BC.

Your dive partner should be able to free you from any entanglement on your gear. If you become separated from your partner, you will need to clear the problem by yourself. If you have a knife and you can reach the line or net, carefully cut it away. It helps to back away from the line to put it under tension. This will make it easier to cut.

Be sure to keep a good grip on your knife so that you don't drop it. When you're serious about wreck diving, you'll probably consider carrying a backup knife as a good investment in your safety.

If you are unable to clear the snag behind you, you may be forced to remove your scuba unit to free it up. Take your time and release your shoulder strap and waist belt while you maintain a grip on your buoyancy compensator and regulator. Once you've cleared the line, you can slip back into your BC.

In addition to the hazards of nets and fishing line, some wrecks may also have exposed electrical wires or cables from the inside of the ship itself, or torn or frayed anchor lines. These hazards can be more difficult to cut than fishing nets or line. If you know or suspect that these types of hazards may exist on a wreck that you plan to dive, it's a good idea to carry a pair of sidecutters to hack through these obstacles.

Cuts from Sharp Metal

When wrecks go to the bottom, they almost invariably are damaged to a certain extent, shearing the sheets of metal that make up the hull, tearing up the railings, and splitting other structures that make up the parts of the ship. These torn metal edges can be as sharp as a razor and will easily tear through most wetsuits and dry suits. Not only can they tear your suit, they can also easily cut your skin.

Although the steel on most wrecks will normally be covered with a deceiving layer of soft rust in salt water, the hard metal underneath may still be razor sharp. Gloves will help protect your hands as will an exposure suit made from a rugged material. Crushed neoprene dry suits are especially popular with wreck divers who explore wrecks in cold water, due to the abrasion resistance of this material. Some divers wear coveralls to help protect their suits.

Wrecks in shallow water that have broken up present a particular hazard in regards to sharp, jagged metal, especially when there are big swells or strong surge. If an unexpected wave moves through the site you could be seriously injured if you are thrown against a piece of sharp or jagged metal. Avoid wrecks in shallow water when diving conditions are poor.

Steel wrecks in shallow water will usually have many jagged surfaces as the wreck breaks up.

Explosive Ordnance

Many of the wrecks that have sunk in military battles are still carrying unexploded artillery shells and small arms ammunition (for machine guns or rifles). While the chance of these munitions exploding appears to be small, these items should be treated as bombs and should not be handled. There is always the possibility that these weapons could detonate causing severe personal injury or death.

Hazards of Wreck Penetration

Wreck penetration, i.e., going inside a wreck beyond the point where daylight is visible, presents many hazards. Entering a wreck and moving beyond the light zone requires special training, equipment, and experience that are beyond the scope of this course. The risks of penetration wreck diving include the danger of becoming lost while you are inside the wreck as well as the possibility of the collapse of the wreck, trapping you inside.

The interior of most wrecks is a maze of unmarked passages that can quickly become quite confusing when you are underwater. Add to the fact that these passages are not lit and usually filled with fine silt that is easily stirred up and you have the makings of a disaster. Many divers have become lost and died inside wrecks due to a lack of proper equipment and training.

One of the more unusual risks in wreck penetration is the danger of col-

It's easy to get lost inside a wreck. Wreck "penetration requires specialized training.

lapse that can occur when a diver breathing compressed air spends a prolonged period inside the wreck. Ships are designed and built to take the stress of compression on their hulls, cabins, and passageways. While a ship is floating, it experiences only this normal strain on its various parts.

When a ship sinks, however, it is subject to stresses that it was never intended to withstand. If a diver enters the wreck, his exhaust bubbles from his regulator will collect in the compartment above him. In a wreck that is old and weakened, if the diver remains in one place for a long time, enough air pressure can be exerted on the overhead "wall" to cause that portion of the wreck to collapse. This type of accident, while not common, has injured and killed divers.

In murky water, it's possible for you to enter part of a wreck without realizing it. In clear water, it's important to avoid the temptation of entering a wreck unless you have the training and equipment to do it properly.

Steel Ships Cause Compass Errors

The magnetic needle in a compass responds to the magnetic north pole of the earth and under normal circumstances, always points in that direction. However, when a compass is surrounded by the steel wreckage of a sunken ship, the compass will become "confused" and not respond properly. If you try to depend on your compass to navigate a wreck site of a steel-hulled ship, you will probably experience navigational errors.

Newer wrecks will cause greater compass errors than older wrecks. As the steel on an older wreck deteriorates, it loses its magnetic pull.

The hull of a steel ship can cause your compass to become "confused."

Fortunately, when you are swimming over a wreck site, the layout of the wreck itself on the bottom will provide you with many visual clues as to your location. This is another reason why it is important to study any drawings or photographs you may have of the wreck so that you will easily be able to orient yourself on the wreck underwater.

Scuba I.Q. Review

It is important for you to learn to identify the risks in wreck diving. If you can answer the following questions, you probably have a good grasp of the potential risks encountered when you explore shipwrecks underwater.

1) List three different potential causes of entanglement that you might encounter while exploring a shipwreck.

2) Why are sport and commercial fishermen attracted to shipwrecks?

3) Explain one reason why shipwrecks in shallow water present a particular hazard when conditions are rough.

4) List two reasons why it is dangerous to penetrate the interior of a shipwreck.

5) Explain why it may be difficult to navigate with a compass on a steel-hulled shipwreck.

Notes:

Chapter 7
Gear for Wreck Diving

Gear for wreck diving can be divided into two categories; i.e., equipment to help you locate a wreck and personal equipment to help increase your safety and enjoyment while wreck diving. The equipment that will help you locate a wreck is not essential unless you are diving from a small boat and attempting to locate a wreck on your own. The personal equipment for wreck diving includes items that will be useful to every diver who explores shipwrecks.

Gear for Locating Shipwrecks

While locating a previously unexplored shipwreck is never easy, modern electronic navigation equipment and surveying devices have made this task much simpler. There are many tools that can help you including charts (paper or electronic), magnetometers, side-scan sonars, fathometers, and metal detectors.

These electronics have dropped enough in price so that many of them are within reach of the serious wreck diver. While the use of these devices is beyond the scope of this book, we'll provide a brief explanation of each of these tools here, since you will probably hear wreck divers discuss these items. Charter vessels that cater to serious wreck divers may be equipped with some or all of these aids to navigation.

Charts

Traditional paper charts are still essential for any type of boating or wreck diving activities, but today there are electronic charts that make these navigational aids much easier to use. In their most common form, electronic charts are integrated with a GPS (Global Positioning System) receiver, that

Paper charts are still important even in the age of electronic aids to navigation.

tracks your boat's location on the water using satellites to calculate your position.

The GPS receiver, which resembles a small electronic game console, displays your location on the screen on an electronic chart that can be "zoomed" in or out to provide more (or less) detail. The exact location of any object can be stored in the GPS unit's memory so that it is easy to return to the same site over and over again.

Magnetometer

A magnetometer is an electronic device that responds to steel objects lying on the bottom underwater. Magnetometers include a topside unit with a display to indicate the presence of any steel objects on the bottom, a cable to connect the display to the sensor or "fish" in the water, and the towed sensor itself. The sensor is pulled along behind the boat until it registers a "hit" or "spike" on the display (or recorder), and the site is marked with either a buoy or by taking a "fix" with a GPS.

Side-Scan Sonar

Side-scan sonar is a device that records the profile of the underwater terrain in detail, making it easy to pick out the distinctive shapes of a shipwrecks. However, as its name implies, a side-scan unit can "look" at the area surrounding the ship that is towing it. It is not limited to searching directly under the boat from which it is being deployed.

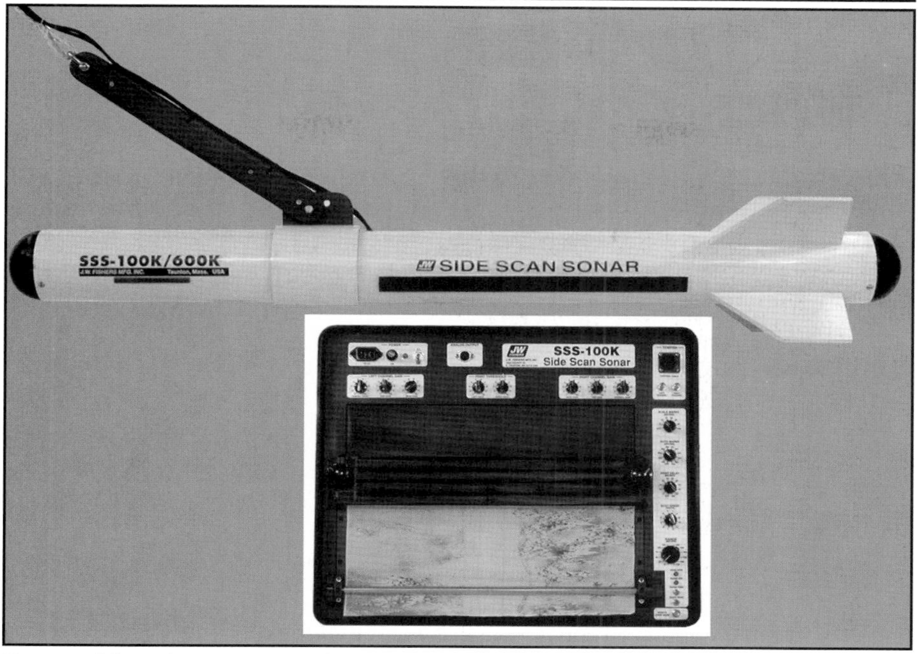

Devices like side scan sonar (top) and proton magnetometers (below) are tools for the serious wreck hunter. (Courtesy J.W. Fishers)

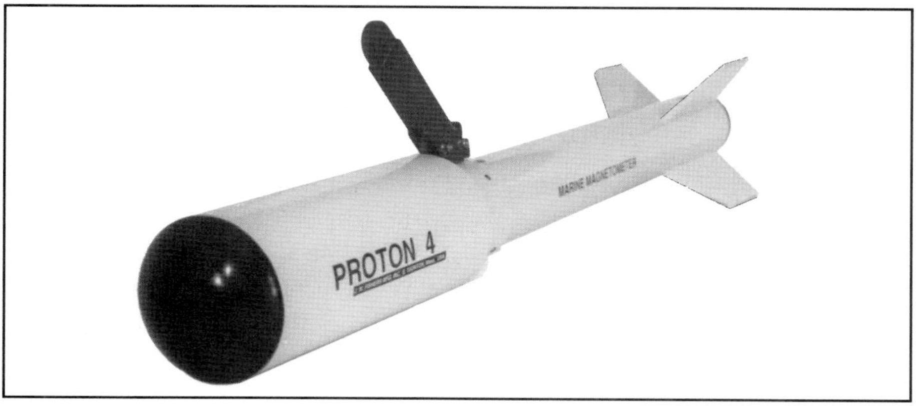

Like a magnetometer, the side-scan system includes a topside control/display box, a cable, and a towed "fish." It takes experience to learn how to operate and adjust a side-scan unit properly.

Fathometer

A fathometer is a device used to measure the depth and profile of the bottom, directly under a boat. These devices are also sometimes referred to as

Metal detectors are used to locate metal objects buried under the sand or encrusted with coral.

"depth finders." Most boats of any size are equipped with fathometers.

Fathometers typically do not provide the detailed information that a side-scan sonar will deliver. However, a fathometer is quite good at showing changes in depth rapidly and simply, which will often help reveal the presence of a shipwreck on an otherwise flat sea bottom.

Metal Detector

Metal detectors are hand-held devices that are used to reveal the presence of metal objects that may be buried beneath the sand or mud on the sea floor, or encrusted with coral or other marine growth. These devices are used primarily by archaeologists and professional salvage teams to help them search for wrecks.

Personal Equipment for Wreck Diving

Personal equipment for wreck diving includes items such as high-performance regulators, bail-out systems, dive lights, knives, and other accessories. Although these items are not essential for sport wreck diving, they are highly recommended.

High-Performance Regulators

Since many wrecks are in deep water, some divers consider a high-performance regulator to be essential for wreck diving. The regulator should have a low work of breathing, meaning that it should not take much effort to either inhale or exhale through the regulator. It should also have a rugged, reliable design.

In addition, be sure to select a regulator that can accommodate a sufficient number of low-pressure accessories including at a minimum a BC inflator, dry suit, and additional second stage. Additional low pressure ports will allow you to route your hoses wherever the least amount of strain on the hoses will occur.

Bail-Out System

A bail-out system is a completely separate and independent breathing system to provide you with emergency air in the event that you run out of air for any reason. The typical bail-out system for sport diving includes a small scuba cylinder (usually 13 cubic feet/2 litres), a regulator, a submersible pressure gauge, and some type of mounting system to attach the cylinder to your primary air supply.

Courtesy of Zeagle Systems, Inc.

An independent bail-out system is the preferred option for an out-of-air emergency.

The use of a bail-out bottle (sometimes referred to as a "pony bottle") and regulator is much preferred to the use of an octopus rig. This allows you to be completely independent of the need to share air with your dive partner in an emergency.

Dive Light

A dive light is a recommended accessory for wreck diving, even during daytime dives. A light will allow you to look back inside "pockets" under the wreck and will reveal the true colors of the marine life on deeper wrecks.

Dive lights need not to be big to be efficient. There are many excellent smaller lights on the market that are more than adequate for recreational wreck diving.

In selecting a light, look for the following features:

- Sinking light – to prevent the light from floating away if you need to set it down.
- Locking switch – to prevent the light from accidentally turning on while it's in your dive bag.
- Long burn time with maximum candlepower
- Rubber shroud – protects front of light from damage
- Lanyard – attaches to your wrist but easily removed in the event of entanglement

Between dives, be sure to avoid leaving your dive light in the sun,

A light is always a useful accessory on a wreck dive.

especially if the weather is hot. The temperature inside the sealed case can get extremely warm and cause the o-ring seal to fail, or your batteries to leak, ruining the light.

Be sure to rinse your dive light with fresh water after each diving day and loosen the battery compartment "door" if you won't be using the light again for awhile. On most lights, the batteries are installed by unscrewing the lens, which also holds the bulb. If you allow the light to sit with the lens screwed down tight, the o-ring may be permanently compressed which could cause your light to leak. When you loosen the lens, if the light is still wet, be sure to turn it upside down so that any water will not run inside the light.

Before you go diving again, remove the lens completely and clean and lubricate the o-ring. Wipe the o-ring with a clean paper towel and clean out the groove where the o-ring sits in the light. Lightly coat the o-ring with a thin film of silicone grease and screw the lens back down until it is snug. The o-ring must be properly installed or the light will flood. Be sure to ask your instructor to show you how to perform this maintenance if you are uncertain of how to do this.

Dive Knife

Any dive knife used for wreck diving must have a sharp blade to enable you to cut through fishing line, rope, or netting easily. You should have at least one knife and preferably two, especially for diving wrecks that are known to be frequented by fishermen.

Your primary knife should have a large blade that has both a straight blade as well as a serrated edge. You can mount this knife on the inside of your calf or on your weight belt.

Your back-up knife can be smaller, but it should still have a sharp blade. Many manufacturers make small knives that can easily be attached to your buoyancy compensator or a low-pressure hose using a special sheath.

One of the trade-offs in selecting a knife is finding a knife that will maintain a sharp edge and that will not rust. Although all dive knives are made of "stainless steel," there are different types of stainless material and almost all will rust. You can help prolong the life of your blade by taking the time to rinse it with fresh water after each diving day, drying it and allowing the sheath to dry, and spraying the blade with a light coat of WD-40® or other anti-corrosion agent. Wipe the blade dry of any excess corrosion inhibitor with a clean cloth or paper towel.

Cutting Devices

Sidecutters, linemen's pliers, or boater's scissors are tools that will cut wire. For a wreck diver, these devices can be an important accessory, since many wrecks are strewn with wires and cables. Some fishing nets are also easier to cut with a pair of sidecutters than with a knife.

To prepare your cutting devices for diving, you'll need to attach a line to it so that you won't lose it. A three foot length of braided nylon line works well for this purpose. Tie a knot around one of the grips on the sidecutters and wrap them tightly, with waterproof electrical tape. Stretch the tape as

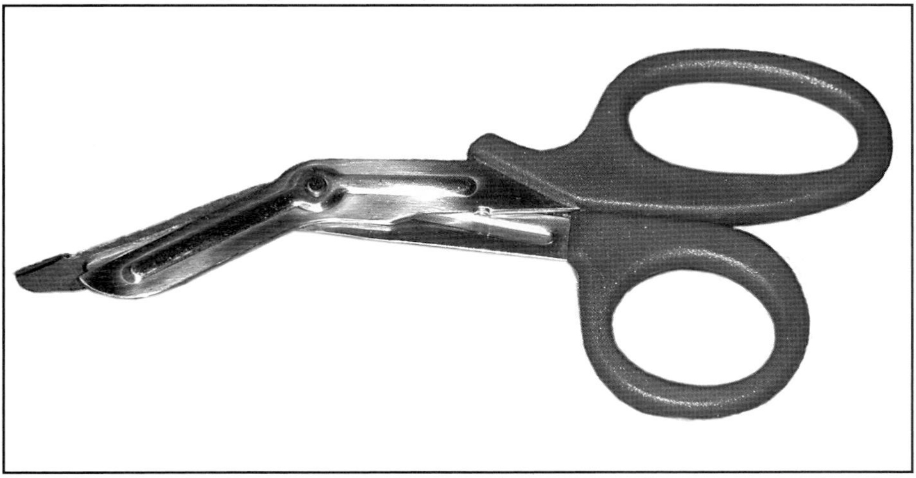

In addition to a kinfe, some type of cutting device that will cut wire or fishing line is recommended for wreck diving. This is a stainless steel pair of "boater's scissors."

you wrap it around the grip and it will adhere better.

Tie a loop in the other end of the nylon line, or connect the line to a brass snap hook that can be connected to a "D" ring on your BC. Some BCs will have rings fastened inside their pockets that can also be used for this purpose. Place the cutting device in your BC pocket where they will be out of the way until you need them.

Since most cutting devies are made of ordinary steel, they will rust when removed from the water. For this reason, it's important to remember to remove them promptly from your BC pocket, rinse them well with fresh water, dry them, and spray them with a corrosion inhibitor.

Underwater Slate

A plastic slate can be extremely useful during any dive, but are particularly useful for wreck diving. You can write on the slate with an ordinary lead pencil. There are also plastic pencils (non-mechanical) that have replaceable lead that work quite well underwater.

The slate can help you to communicate with your dive partner, but for wreck exploration, its main function is to help you map the wreck so that you better understand how the site is laid out on the bottom. You can use either a wrist slate or a flat slate, although a flat slate tends to work better for drawing the features of a large or widely scattered wreck.

The more detailed your notes, the easier it will be to map out the wreck so that you know where everything lies. The larger the wreck and the deeper the water, the more time it will take you to see the entire wreck and com-

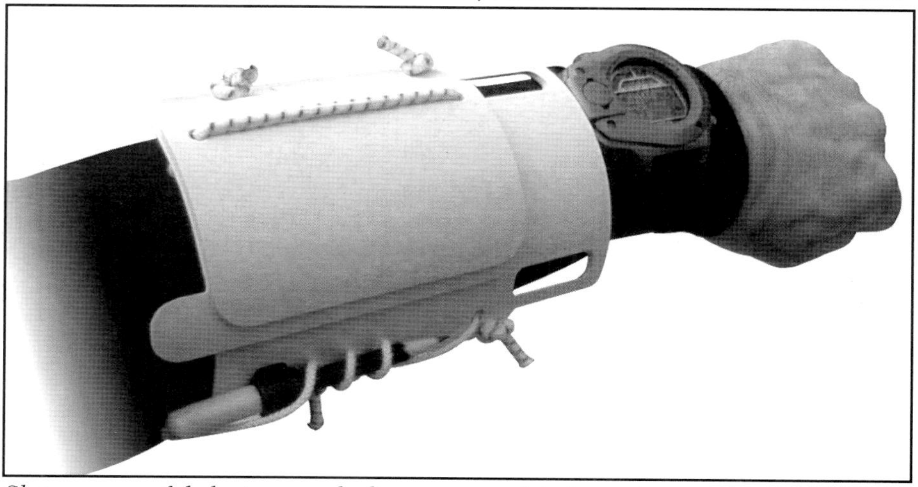

Photo courtesy of Dive-Rite

Slates are useful during wreck dives to record information on the layout of the wreck.

plete your sketch.

To clean your slate, use a plastic scouring pad with an abrasive cleaner. You can also use an ordinary eraser, but a scouring pad and cleaner are much more effective.

Wreck Reel

Although reels are used primarily for penetration dives inside wrecks or caves, they can also be useful for exploring the exposed portions of a wreck, particularly on a site where the visibility is poor and the wreck is broken up. Learning how to use a reel effectively is not difficult but it does take a little practice.

Most underwater reels are made of stainless steel, brass, or plastic parts. They are designed to be hand-held but can be clipped to your BC when not in use. The crank should be large and easily gripped with gloves. The reel must also have a lock to prevent line from feeding out when the reel is not in use.

Most reels are rigged with several hundred feet (60-90 metres) of braided nylon line. You can attach a brass snap hook or other similar type of fastener to the free end of the line so that it is simple to attach the line to the wreck.

Reels should be rinsed with fresh water at the end of each diving day, and any metal parts should be sprayed with a light coating of corrosion inhibiting

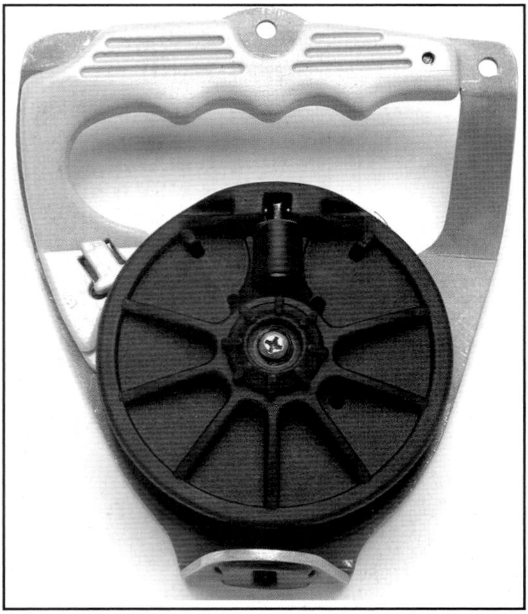

The use of a reel can greatly increase your safety on a wreck. (photo courtesy of Scubapro)

spray to keep the reel turning smoothly. The line must be replaced whenever it shows signs of wear. If the line breaks while you are underwater, you could find it difficult or impossible to return to your starting point on the bottom

Marker Buoy

If you are diving a new wreck, and you have just located it for the first time, you may want to use a marker buoy to identify the central portion of the wreck, or other key points, to which you want to return. The buoy can be used to take surface fixes, too, by using either visual line-ups (triangulation) or using electronic navigation instruments, such as GPS.

Buoys for use underwater usually consist of some type of small float, 100 feet (30 metres) or more of braided white nylon line or polypropylene, and a small weight to compensate for the buoyancy of the float. Since polypropylene floats it tends to work better underwater and the line has less of a tendency to end up in a knotted mass. A brass snap hook may be used to attach the marker buoy to your buoyancy compensator, or depending on the size of the marker, it may fit in your BC pocket.

When you're finished using the buoy, tightly wind the line back onto it, and rinse it with fresh water. Store it out of the sun to help avoid deterioration.

By using a marker buoy, it becomes very easy to return to any portion of the wreck you wish to explore on a subsequent dive. (photo courtesy of OMS).

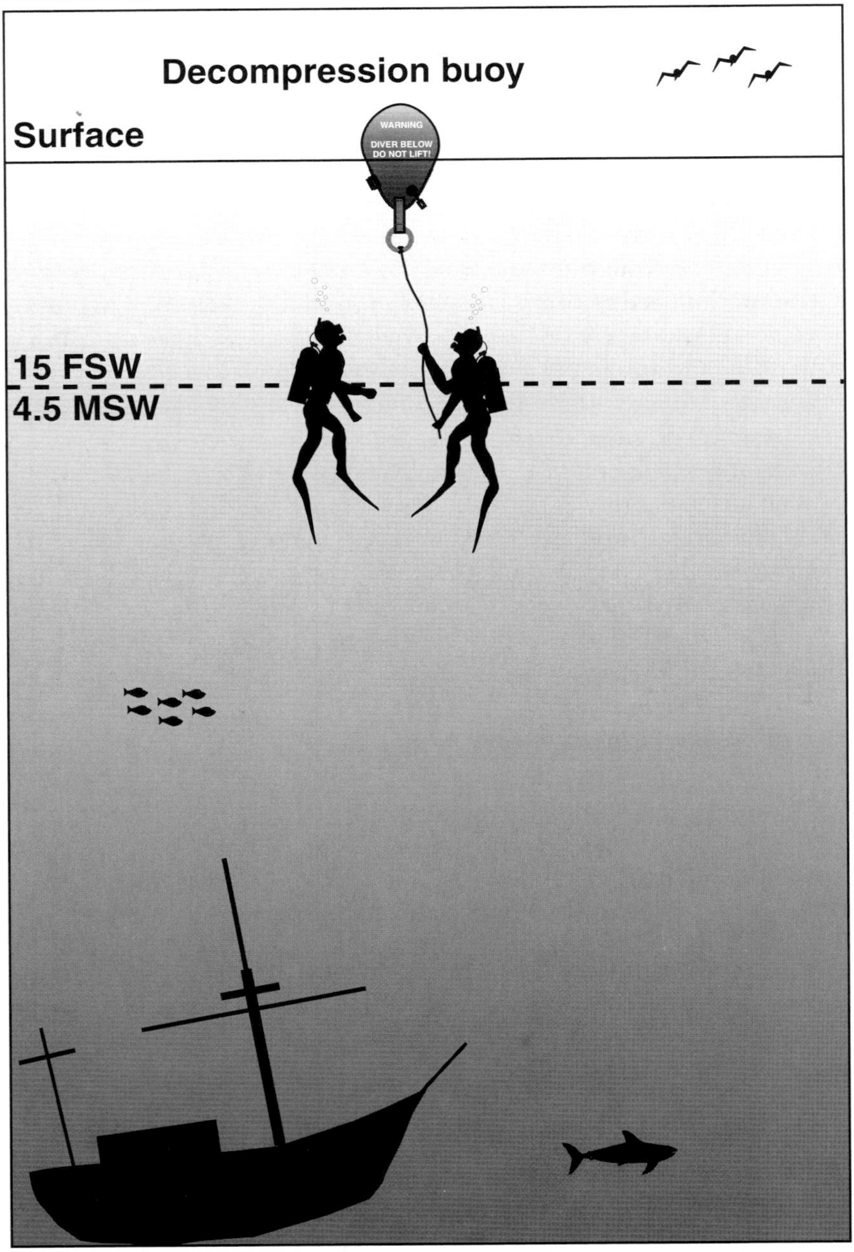

A decompression buoy can greatly increase your safety in the event that there are strong currents that make it difficult to complete your safety stop over the wreck itself.

Up-Line Reel and Float

If you regularly dive wrecks in deep water, far from shore, you may sometimes find yourself in a situation where the boat either drags its anchor off the wreck or the anchor breaks free. In either case, these situations usually arise to sudden changes in weather.

In a situation where you return to the spot where the anchor was fixed, only to find it gone, there is no substitute for an "up-line reel" and/or a float (buoy). This allows you to make a safety stop (precautionary decompression stop) without the need to hover in mid-water.

Divers may use a variety of reels underwater to assist them in making safety stops when the boat has pulled off site or if they were unable to return to the anchor underwater, if the boat has dragged anchor or the anchor line has been severed. In situations where there is no strong current, you fasten your line to the wreck and unreel it as you make your ascent to your safety stop. When you are at the appropriate depth for your stop, you inflate the lift bag to mark your position. Once you have completed your stop, you release the line, surface, deflate the bag, and signal the boat to pick you up.

The preferred type of line to be used on a reel for this application is manila, which is a natural fiber line that will eventually disintegrate underwater, leaving no trace of their existence. This is preferred over nylon lines which will last for many years.

If manila is used it must be wetted down and stretched before it is used on a reel. If it is not, there is a good chance it will constrict and knot itself into a ball, making it very difficult to handle.

Scuba I.Q. Review

Wreck diving is much easier and more enjoyable when you are properly equipped. Be prepared to discuss your equipment needs with your instructor by reviewing the following questions.

1) List three pieces of electronic equipment that can be used to help locate shipwrecks.

2) Explain the purpose of a bail-out system and list its component parts.

3) List three features that are desirable in a dive light.

4) Explain why sidecutters may be a useful accessory for wreck diving.

5) List two uses for an underwater slate during a wreck dive.

6) Explain the proper use of a reel during a wreck dive.

7) Explain the proper use of a marker buoy during a wreck dive.

8) Define the term "up-line reel" and explain how this device is used.

Notes:

Chapter 8
Planning Wreck Dives

A well thought out plan for a wreck dive is crucial to making your wreck diving experience a success, especially if the dive is deep, visibility is low, the water is cold, or there are other challenging environmental factors. It takes time and experience to develop a good dive plan, and plans tend to work best when each member of the dive team has contributed to the project.

In this chapter, we'll examine the elements that you should consider when putting together your wreck diving plan. We'll look at the layout of the wreck, your equipment, the personnel, and your objectives, along with other factors critical to your preparations.

Consider the Wreck Site

All aspects of the wreck site itself should be considered when putting together your dive plan. The layout of the wreck will have a major impact on your dive plan. Elements that you must consider include the following:

• Is the wreck intact or is it broken up and widely scattered?

It's much easier to explore an intact wreck than one that is widely scattered across the bottom. Sometimes it's difficult to locate all the pieces of a wreck that has been broken up and strewn for a long distance across the bottom.

• How big is the wreck?

It takes more time to explore a large wreck than a small one. Some wrecks are so big that it's impossible to see the whole wreck in a single dive. In this case, it's usually better to concentrate on a specific portion of the wreck on each dive.

The condition of the wreck will greatly affect your dive and the plan for it. Although this doesn't look much like a wreck site, the the diver in this photo is exploring the wreck of the Winnfield Scott, off the coast of California.

• Is the wreck right side up, upside down, or lying on its side?

Not all wrecks go straight to the bottom and land sitting upright. Some ships "turn turtle" when they go down or "list" on the bottom depending on the terrain. It can be very disorienting to explore a wreck that is upside down or lying on its side. If the wreck is upside down, many parts of it will be inaccessible.

• Are different parts of the wreck at various depths?

Some wrecks are located on sloping bottoms so that parts of the wreck may be quite shallow, while others are at depths that exceed the maximum recommended sport diving range. It's usually best to try to dive the deepest portions of the wreck first, to maximize your bottom time.

• Is the wreck relatively recent or is it old?

Older, scattered wrecks may be so overgrown with marine life that they can be difficult to recognize as wrecks. They may be encrusted with growth, or buried under mud or sand. You must train your eye to look for straight lines or other man-made shapes that reveal the presence of the wreck.

• Are there any unusual hazards at the site?

If the wreck is popular with fishermen, there will almost certainly be nets and lines that have been lost on the ship. In this situation it is essential that everyone is equipped with a dive knife, and sidecutters are strongly recommended.

As mentioned previously, some wrecks are located in areas where there are strong currents, heavy surge, or other environmental factors. Low visibility may also be a problem. Some wrecks may contain cargo that can be hazardous, such as chemicals or unexploded munitions (gun shells).

What is the Objective of the Dive?

As you formulate your plan, one of the first questions that you must answer is, "What is your objective?" If your goal is to take pictures during the dive, then you don't want to be burdened with a goody bag for capturing lobsters on the same dive. Both you and your dive partner should have the same objective for the dive.

The best dive plans are the simplest, i.e., those that have a single objective as their focus. If your goal is to take photos of the propellers on the stern in 130 FSW (40 metres), you probably won't have time to explore the bow of the ship on the same dive. Don't try to do it all in a single dive.

Once you have defined your objective for the dive, many of the other elements of your dive plan will automatically fall into place. It will be much easier to determine what gear you need or what time of day you should make your dive.

Equipment Needs

It's important to obtain any special equipment that you may need well in advance of the dive and to rig it properly for use. Be sure to test any new piece of equipment prior to using it on a critical dive. If you will be using a new piece of gear, such as a reel, it's a good idea to practice using it under less demanding conditions than those you might encounter during your first deep wreck dive in cold water.

Decide exactly what gear you will need for the dive and leave behind any items that aren't required. You don't want to be burdened with excess gear that won't be needed.

Who is on the Dive Team?

Almost anyone can explore a simple wreck in warm, clear, shallow water where there is no current. However, with more demanding environmental factors, the amount of training and experience you need to properly and confidently participate in wreck diving increases.

Wrecks that have been deliberately sunk for diving usually have access holes cut in them so that divers can swim through them in relative safety, without ever leaving the zone of available light. This access should be discussed as part of your dive plan.

To explore shipwrecks, ideally, you want to dive with a partner who matches your level of training and experience. If you meet a new potential dive partner, you will want to discuss your respective diving backgrounds together before making a more difficult wreck dive. You'll also want to examine their equipment to make sure they are properly equipped, that all of their equipment is functional, and that you understand how to operate their releases and other aspects of their gear. Check to be certain that you both use the same hand signals and discuss any special signals that you may want to use for the dive.

You should fully discuss all aspects of the dive plan with your dive partner to ensure that you both are in agreement about how the dive is to be conducted and under what conditions you will terminate the dive. If you can't agree on how the dive is to be conducted you need to look for another dive partner.

The divemaster should also be an experienced wreck diver and preferably one who has experience diving the particular wreck that you are planning to explore. In some cases, the divemaster may lead the dive, while in other situations the divemaster may remain on board to check people in and out of the water and to serve in a support capacity.

Under certain conditions, the divemaster may "stagger" the number of divers entering the water at any one time. This practice is common especially on smaller wrecks and may be used on deeper wrecks, too. On a small wreck, staggering the divers reduces the number of divers on the wreck itself, so that everyone can experience a more enjoyable dive. On deeper wrecks, staggering the divers reduces the number of divers at depth for safety purposes and makes the anchor line (or deco bar) less crowded during safety stops.

If you're not among the first group of divers to enter the water, it's important to be sure that you are ready to go when it's your turn to dive. If there are other divers following you, you don't want to be the one to hold them up and cut down on their dive time.

When will you dive?

A big part of your planning should take into consideration both the date of your dive and the time of day. The date of your dive will determine the phase of the moon and may play the biggest role in your ability to dive since tidal changes and currents may make certain wrecks inaccessible. You'll want to consult the tide tables well in advance of any planned trip to determine the best possible days to dive and the time of the tides on the day you plan to dive.

In many locations, you'll want to start your dive on the flood (rising)

Underwater visibility has a huge impact on wreck diving. In low visibility, it may be difficult to see enough of a large object to understand what part of the wreck you have located. This diver is examining a capstan winch, used to raise the anchor on an old sailing ship.

tide, just prior to high tide, since this is when the water will usually be the clearest. In addition, tidal flow will be slowing.Wreck diving usually requires "slack water." This varies according to your location, but can be predicted by using tide tables.

The season of the year will also have a big impact on underwater visibility and sea conditions in many locations. For example, in the Caribbean, the summer months will usually provide the clearest water and best weather conditions. Hurricane season in the Caribbean begins in late summer, however, and continues through the fall. Early summer plankton blooms will reduce visibility and light penetration.

Dive Boats for Wreck Diving

In many parts of the world there are dive boats that cater to wreck divers. In most cases, there are no physical differences in the boats themselves compared to other dive boats in the same area. However, the boat may be equipped with additional electronics and the crew will be extremely knowledgeable about location and history of the wrecks themselves, equipment for wreck diving, and procedures.

Boat crews and captains who specialize in wreck diving trips understand the importance of placing divers right on the wreck at the start of their dive. In some cases, the boat will anchor directly into the wreck itself, but in other situations, the anchor will be dropped next to the wreck. Most wrecks that have been sunk deliberately for diving will have mooring buoys on or next to them to avoid anchor damage to the wreck itself.

Contingency Planning

A good dive plan will always include procedures and preparation for all reasonably foreseeable emergencies. You need to decide in advance what types of situations you can deal with underwater and what types of situations will prompt you to terminate a dive.

As we've already mentioned, the two potential emergencies that should be considered in wreck diving are the possibility of entanglement and accidental penetration of the wreck. Of these, accidental penetration of the wreck would usually be the more serious situation.

Entanglement

In most cases, entanglement can typically be dealt with rather easily. You should be able to pull the entanglement close to you and cut it with your knife. Your dive partner should normally be close enough to see that you are having a problem and they should be able to assist you.

The worst case would be an entanglement behind you that restricts your ability to turn and your dive partner is unavailable. In this situation, your only option is to slip out of your scuba unit and to cut it free.

Wreck Penetration

In low visibility, it's entirely possible to accidentally swim inside a part of a wreck without realizing it. If this happens, you could become lost inside the wreck This type of accident is uncommon, but what's more typical is the diver who is not trained for wreck diving but decides to enter a wreck anyway.

Most wrecks that have been underwater for any length of time have a great deal of fine silt inside them. Unless you are familiar with "non-silting techniques," it's almost a given that you will stir up the silt and reduce visibility to zero. It can take a long time for the silt to settle out, sometimes much longer than the remaining air in a scuba cylinder.

If you find yourself lost inside a wreck, it is essential that you attempt to remain calm and attempt to conserve your air by breathing slowly and rhythmically. Chances are, if your entrance to the wreck was accidental, you probably did not penetrate the wreck too far before realizing your mistake.

If you find yourself lost inside a wreck, your only option is to attempt to try to retrace your steps and/or hope that someone with the right training and gear will realize that you are lost and come to your rescue.

Occasionally if you enter a wreck by accident there is a tendency to use your light to search for the exit point. It is quicker to settle yourself, switch the light off and look around for the dim aura of ambient light filtering through the darkness. This usually leads you back to an entry point safely and quickly.

Scuba I.Q. Review

Dive planning for wreck diving requires a bit more thought than most other types of recreational dives. Discuss the plan for your dives during this course with your instructor. Use the questions listed below as the basis for your discussion.

1) List four aspects of a wreck site that must be considered when preparing your dive plan.

2) Explain why both you and your dive partner should have the same objective for your dive plan.

3) State the two conditions that might cause a divemaster to stagger the entry times of a group of divers participating in a wreck dive.

4) List two reasons why it is important to take tides into consideration when planning a dive.

5) Define the term "wreck penetration" and explain why this procedure is not recommended for sport divers.

Notes:

Sting

Chapter 9
Making Wreck Dives

In the excitement of gearing up to make a wreck dive, it's all too easy to let your enthusiasm overwhelm your safety. Competition with other divers – whether it's to be first on the wreck, or to explore some new portion of the site – can also interfere with good judgment on a wreck dive. The experienced and knowledgeable diver makes a point of slow, methodical preparation, so that nothing is unplanned and no contingency is unanticipated.

Down to the Wreck

The descent to a new wreck can be one of the most exciting highlights of the dive, especially when the visibility is good and you can see a good portion of the wreck lying below you on the bottom.

If the visibility is poor, the wreck may not materialize in your sight until you are very close to it. This can be disorienting if you aren't exactly sure of what part of the wreck you have landed on.

As you make your descent, and once you have reached the wreck, pay particular attention to the direction of the current and the angle and direction of the sun. Both of these physical aspects of the dive will provide you with directional clues to help you navigate the site. Also, be sure to take note of the location of the anchor, especially if it is in a location that is at all different from where you expected it to be.

On the Wreck

Once you've reached the wreck, take a moment to orient yourself and be sure you understand where you have made contact with the ship. This is especially important if visibility is low and you could not see a large portion

It takes practice to use a reel properly and skillfully for wreck diving. If you don't practice, a reel can be more of a liability than an asset.

of the wreck during your descent.

Using Your Reel

If the wreck is mostly intact, there's usually not much reason to use a reel, unless you just want to practice your skills. Where the reel is most useful is in helping you maintain an orientation to the anchor when visibility is poor or on a wreck that is badly broken up and scattered.

If you're using a reel, the first thing that you'll want to do is to fasten it off to a secure location. Be sure to take a moment to select a good connecting point for the line since a poor location could lead to the line getting cut or make it difficult to pay the line out or retrieve it.

To use the reel, clip the free end off to a heavy piece of wreckage near the anchor on the bottom. Allow the line to slowly unspool as you swim out away from the anchor.

If the visibility is good and you can see there are no major obstructions on the bottom, you can swim a wedge shaped pattern of exploration along the bottom away from the anchor line, but you must take care not to swim a circle around the anchor. If the wreck lies low to the bottom you will be able to explore a large swath of the site, provided your reel line doesn't hang up on any high profile wreckage.

If the wreck has a lot of "relief," i.e., parts of the wreck stand high above the bottom, you will need to swim back to where the line is tied off and swim out at a different angle away from your starting point to see other parts of the wreck. When the visibility is poor, you'll probably need to concentrate on swimming a relatively straight line and you will be limited to exploring only a portion of the wreck.

As you pay the line out, try to avoid obstructions that the line can snag on so that when it's time to reel the line back in, you don't have to waste time freeing the line. You should strive to maintain a continuous tension on the line to help avoid the line becoming entangled in the wreck. If the line drops into a narrow slot between large, jagged pieces of wreckage, it can be difficult to free it, or it could be cut.

Under most circumstances you'll want to "anchor" the line periodically to other pieces of wreckage. This will help prevent the line from becoming entangled in areas where you don't want it to go. You can do this by taking a wrap or two around a small but immovable item. Don't rig your line to pieces of wreckage that are so lightweight that you could drag them across the bottom.

By using multiple tie-off points you'll be able to change direction more easily. Just be sure to allow yourself enough time to disconnect your line and still get back to the anchor line with sufficient leeway without incurring a decompression obligation.

Exploring the Wreck

As you swim along the wreck, be sure to watch for lines and nets. Also keep an eye out for sharp or twisted metal. If there is a strong current, it is often easier to pull yourself along the wreck than to try to swim against the current.

If the wreck has open compartments that you can enter without moving beyond the point where natural light can be seen, you may cautiously enter these areas. This exploration of areas that are lit by natural light should not be confused with "penetration dives."

Proper buoyancy control and "trim" are especially important while exploring any shipwreck. Most open water divers never give much thought to trim, but this is an extremely important consideration in many types of diving. Trim is defined as the angle at which you swim through the water.

Basically, there are three different types of trim that divers commonly use. "Head-up" trim (or positive trim) is the most common trim angle, where you swim through the water with your head higher (shallower) than your feet. Neutral trim is when you swim through the water with your head and feet at the same depth. You are practicing "head-down" trim (or negative trim) when you swim through the water with your head lower than your feet.

Any space that is even partially enclosed in a wreck is subject to the accumulation of fine silt that will cover the bottom of the compartment. If you are careless about your buoyancy and trim you'll stir up this silt, potentially reducing visibility to zero. In order to avoid this problem, you need to swim with head-down trim. It can take hours for any silt that is in the water to settle out to the bottom.

If the wreck has a steel hull, you'll want to limit your contact with the wreck as much as possible to avoid having rust from the wreck stain your dive gear.

Understanding What You're Seeing

The more you know about ship design from the era that the wreck was built, the more you will understand what you're looking at underwater. It really helps to have studied any drawings or photos of the wreck that may be available.

Keep in mind that even if you dive a wreck frequently and think you know the wreck, the site can and will change over time. The changes may be very gradual, especially for a wreck in deep water, where the only disturbance

Watch out for jagged pieces of metal when you explore a wreck.

The more you know about a wreck, the better you will understand the parts you see.

to the wreck may be the corrosion of the parts. Conversely, changes can be sudden and violent, especially on a shallow wreck, where storms can tumble loose parts, or waves can do great damage. In addition, parts of the wreck that are buried in the sand can be uncovered after a violent storm, or buried as sands shift during the summer.

Marine growth on wrecks can also change the appearance of the wreck, making parts of it unrecognizable. Coral, kelp, encrusting worms, and other organisms can all change the appearance of wreck.

Using a Marker Buoy

If you're diving a wreck for the first time, and you didn't anchor directly on the wreck, you may want to use a marker buoy to indicate its location. This will allow you to take a compass or GPS fix directly on top of the wreck. You can use your marker to identify specific features of the wreck if you want to return to them on the next dive to take a photo or do a sketch.

To use the buoy, it should be clipped off to the wreckage and only enough line should be unspooled to reach the surface, plus enough additional to compensate for any tidal change or currents. The line should be knotted back on itself or snapped into the line retainer on the buoy to help prevent all of the line upspooling from the float before it is released.

When you're done using a buoy, don't waste your bottom time reeling up the line while you're underwater. Disconnect the anchor for the buoy and make sure it won't become tangled in the wreck, but allow it to remain near the bottom. Wind the line back on the buoy on the surface while the anchor keeps the line extended so it won't get knotted up. Wrap the line tightly back on the buoy the same way it was wrapped when you first used it.

Never leave a buoy on a wreck any longer than absolutely necessary. The line can become entangled in a passing boat's propeller and you could be liable for any damage. Even if the buoy does not wrap around a boat's prop, the line could be severed and the buoy lost. Buoys left on a wreck may also be taken by other divers who may think that you have abandoned the buoy.

Using an Up-Line Reel and Buoy

If you get back to the anchor and find that it is not there, you may need to use your reel to make your ascent. You can use your reel provided there is not a strong current. Your instructor will recommend how to deploy the reel according to local practices.

When there is no strong current, you can make your safety stop on the line attached to the bottom. If you fasten your line off to the wreck, do not

Proper buoyancy control is extremely important in all diving and especially during wreck diving.

attach it to any part of the wreck that might be damaged or break loose.

If the current is strong, you may need to use your decompression buoy to make your safety stop. In this situation you do not anchor the up-line reel to the wreck, but ascend to a depth of 15-20 FSW (5-6.5 metres) and inflate the decompression buoy. Once the buoy is inflated, you can hang beneath it. Keep in mind that the current will carry you away from the wreck. You must be equipped with surface signaling equipment in the event that the boat does not see your buoy and you drift away from the site. Without proper signaling gear, i.e., an air horn or visual devices, you could be lost at sea.

In a situation where you are making your ascent on your own line, it is essential that you have a completely independent back-up air supply for use during your safety stop or for emergency decompression in the event that you have overstayed your bottom time. Without an auxiliary supply you will be placing yourself at risk.

Some divers will fasten the up-line or decompression buoy to their harness. This procedure is only acceptable provided that you are using a quick-release snap shackle (not a brass snap-hook) to disconnect the line in the event of an emergency.

Keeping an Eye on the Weather

Many ships sink due to heavy weather conditions. If you are diving a wreck where the weather is known to deteriorate quickly with little advance warning, it's essential to pay attention to changes in the weather during the course of the day. The same conditions that made the wreck that you are diving sink could also endanger your boat if you are not careful.

Scuba I.Q. Review

Before your first wreck dive, take a few moments to discuss the following questions with your instructor.

1) What are two physical aspects of the diving environment that can help you navigate on a shipwreck.

2) List two situations where a wreck diving reel is useful.

3) Describe the procedure for using a reel while exploring a shipwreck.

4) Define the term "trim" as it applies to scuba diving.

5) List the three different types of trim and which one is most desirable when exploring a partially enclosed compartment on a shipwreck.

6) List two different factors that can change the physical appearance of a shipwreck.

7) State two reasons why a marker buoy should not be left on a wreck any longer than necessary.

8) Explain the procedures for using an up-line reel and decompression buoy.

Chapter 10
Extending Your Diving Capabilities

Boat diving, drift diving, and wreck diving open the door to many exciting diving possibilities. These three specialty areas provide a good jumping off point to extend your diving capabilities and horizons. In this chapter we'll discuss some of the other specialty and technical diving courses that can take you to new depths.

Nitrox

Nitrox is a term that covers any gas mixture that contains more than the usual 21% oxygen found in normal air. Divers use nitrox in order to extend their bottom time at diving depths down to 130 FSW (40 metres).

By increasing the amount of oxygen in the gas you breathe underwater (and decreasing the nitrogen) we gain a great deal of bottom time at sport diving depths. The higher the percentage of oxygen in the air, the longer we can stay at any given depth, although there are depth limits for each specific nitrox mixture.

Common nitrox mixtures contain anywhere from 32% oxygen up to 60% oxygen, but the most popular mixtures are mixtures containing 32%, 36%, and 40% oxygen. SDI instructors teach an introductory nitrox course that will prepare you to use mixtures containing up to, and including, 40% oxygen. Technical Diving International (TDI) runs courses that prepare you to use nitrox mixtures containing over 40% oxygen.

If you want to maximize your bottom time, nitrox diving is for you!

Advanced Wreck Diving

It takes special equipment, training, and preparation to enter an intact shipwreck. In the advanced wreck diving course, you will further the skills

Nitrox can help to extend the amount of time you can spend underwater exploring shipwrecks.

you learned in your introductory wreck diver training. You'll learn more about how to use reels, back-up equipment, and special techniques for rigging your gear. You'll also learn more about "non-silting" techniques for exploring the most remote parts of any wreck.

As an advanced wreck diver, you'll be able to discover places that most divers never get to see. If shipwrecks excite you, this course will give you the tools to expand your adventures beyond the ordinary!

Semi-Closed Circuit Rebreather

A rebreather is a type of scuba system that "recycles" each breath you exhale, so that very little breathing gas is wasted. The rebreather removes the carbon dioxide from your exhaled breath and adds fresh oxygen to the gas mixture. By recapturing your exhaled breathing gas, the rebreather is extremely efficient in its gas utilization. A small cylinder of nitrox can last a rebreather diver up to 120 minutes.

Besides their efficient use of breathing gas, rebreathers also have other advantages over ordinary scuba. Because they give off little or no exhaust bubbles, rebreathers are much quieter than ordinary scuba gear, making it possible to get close to certain marine creatures, such as the hammerhead sharks found off Cocos Island and in the Sea of Cortez. In addition, rebreathers provide warm, moist breathing gas, a decided advantage in cold water diving.

Rebreathers are ideal equipment for wreck divers, underwater photographers, and small boat owners.

Decompression Diving

Decompression diving will train you to make planned decompression dives at depths down to 150 FSW (45 metres). In this course you'll learn how to calculate and manage your breathing gas needs and select the best decompression mix for your dives.

Since many wrecks are in the depth range where decompression is required to make a dive with any meaningful bottom time, this course is essential for divers who don't want to restrict their ability to explore more challenging sites.

Extended Range Diving

Extended range diving encompasses dives using compressed air that go beyond the 130 FSW (40 metres) traditional sport diving depth limit down

Semi-closed circuit rebreathers are a great way to enhance the benefits of nitrox diving.

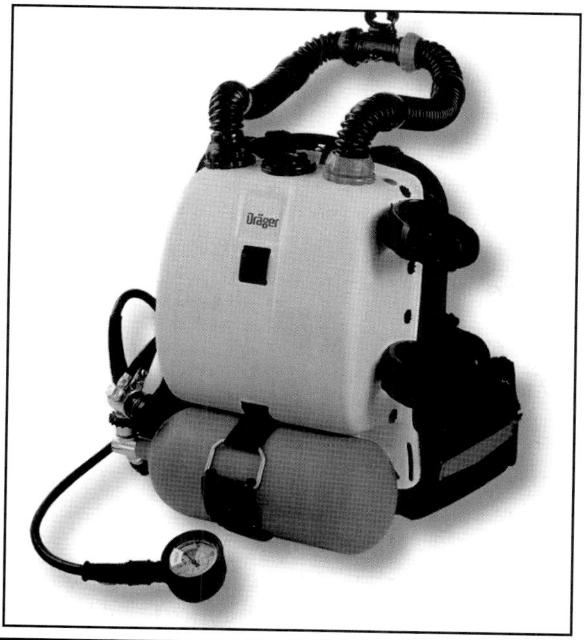

to 180 FSW (55 metres). In addition, during these dives, decompression using nitrox mixtures or pure oxygen is performed. Many deeper wrecks fall in this depth range.

Tri-Mix Diving

Tri-mix is a mixture of three gases, including helium, nitrogen, and oxygen. Divers use tri-mix because by replacing some of the nitrogen in the gas mixture with helium, the intoxication cause by nitrogen at deeper depths is greatly reduced. Tri-mix diving is considered to be the most sophisticated form of deep diving practiced today.

Tri-mix can be used effectively at any depth beyond 130 FSW (40 metres), although it is most popular for dives below 165 FSW (50 metres). Many deep wreck dives today are made with tri-mix.

Photo courtesy of OMS.

Tri-mix allows divers to explore deeper wrecks with increased efficiency and sophistication.

Scuba I.Q. Review

There are many other diving specialty courses that you can participate in after you complete your current training. Talk with your instructor about the special types of diving that interest you and decide which additional training courses suit your needs. Review the following questions to help you decide which type of courses you want to take.

1) Define the term "nitrox."

2) List two topics that are covered in an advanced wreck diving course.

3) List two of the advantages of using a semi-closed circuit rebreather.

4) Define the term "tri-mix" and explain why this breathing gas is often used for deep dives beyond 130 FSW (40 metres).

Additional Reading

Berg, Dan. *Shipwreck Diving, A Complete Diver's Handbook to Mastering the Skills of Wreck Diving*. Aqua Explorers, New York, NY. 88 pages, 1991

Keats, Henry and Skerry, Brian. *Complete Wreck Diving: A Guide to Diving Wrecks*. Aqua Quest Publications, New York, NY. 2002

Marx, Robert. *In the Wake of Galleons*. Best Publishing, Flagstaff, AZ. 418 pages, 2001

About SDI and TDI

About TDI

TDI was formed in 1994 by some of diving's most experienced instructors to bring technical applications of the sport to a wider audience. TDI's library of training materials and texts have become known as the industry's best and most professional resources. Most importantly, TDI has the best safety record of all training agencies.

Whether your interests lie in nitrox, rebreathers, mixed gas or any of the many other programs that TDI offers, you can be assured that you will be participating in training that offers you the "cutting edge" of diving technology. With offices worldwide and over 10,000 instructors teaching our programs, TDI has become the largest international specialized dive agency.

About SDI

SDI grew out of the success of our sister company TDI, which specialized in more advanced disciplines of dive training. Our instructors asked for an entry level scuba training program that would reflect that same forward-looking approach that TDI brought to technical diving pursuits.

Finally after a year in development, the SDI training program was launched at the 1999 DEMA show. It was an instant success on its own merits. Both students and instructors have embraced the no nonsense approach that the SDI training system offers. We have streamlined the course materials to let students study the essential academics with a renewed emphasis on practical diving skills learned in both the pool and open water environments. SDI was the first to require students to be taught with modern dive computers from the outset.

Diving is constantly changing. Many other agencies are still mired in yesterday while our staff looks ahead to the millennium and strives to continue our record as the innovators of the industry. We want to make the experience of diving one that is enjoyed by every family member to the fullest. At SDI we are all divers and want to share our love of the sport with as wide an audience as possible. Please check out the variety of programs at SDI and join us in our passion!

SDI DIVER PROGRAMS

SCUBA DIVING INTERNATIONAL

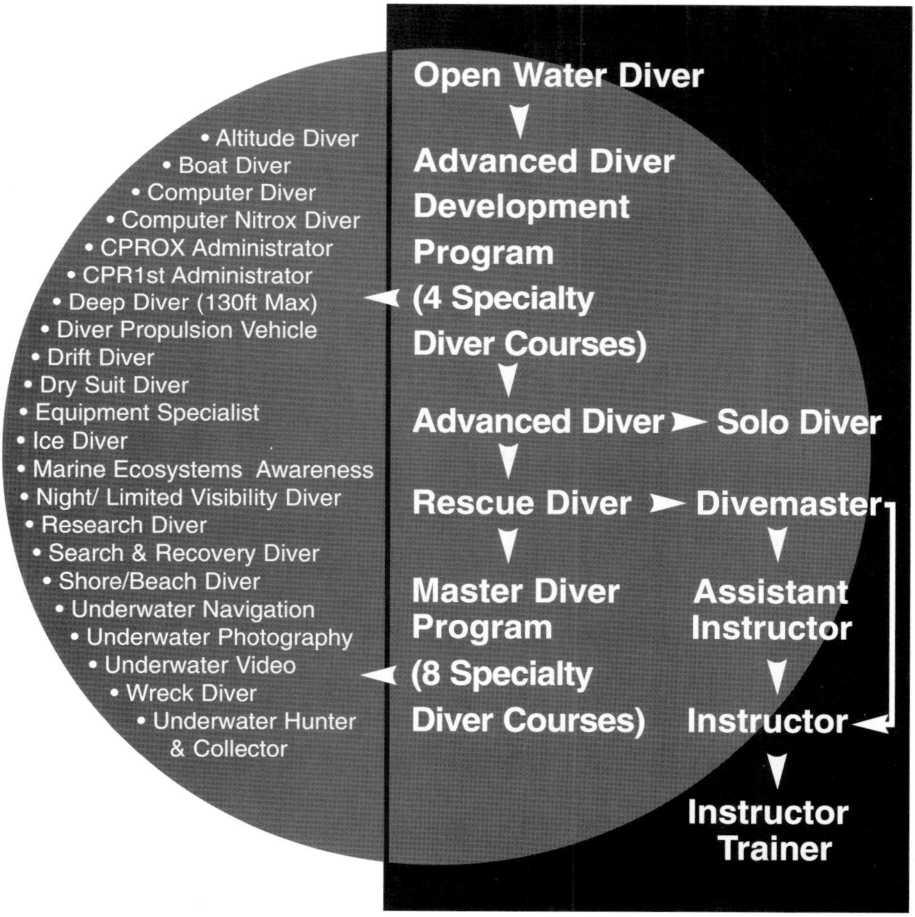

Glossary

alpha flag – a blue and white flag that is used to signify that a boat is conducting diving operations.

anchor locker – where the anchor is stored.

anchor windlass – a mechanical device used to raise or lowe the anchor. May also be referred to as a winch.

aft deck – the area on the deck behind the ship's superstructure.

bail-out system – a set of diving equipment that is designed to provide a diver with an emergency air supply completely independent of his primary breathing system

bow – The front of the boat.

bridge – the location on a large ship from which the vessel is steered and controlled.

broach – when a boat turns sideways to the seas and rolls over

bunk – a bed on a ship

capstan – a type of winch where the drum that the line turns on is oriented vertically

cleat – a fitting on the deck of a ship that is used to fasten lines to.

cuddy cabin – a small cabin on a boat

debris field – the area

drift dive – a planned dive that starts in one location, where the diver is carried by the current, and ends at another completely different location, at a considerable distance from the start point.

EPIRB – acronym that stands for Emergency Position Indicating Radio

Beacon. Used by mariners whose boat has sunk to signal to rescue agencies that they need assistance.

fathomter – a device that is carried aboard a boat and used to measure the water depth directly under the boat. May also be referred to as a "depth sounder."

freeboard – distance from the deck o a boat to the water.

FSW – feet of sea water

galley – where the food is prepared.

hang-off line – a line that is used to support any gear that you don't want to carry while you are entering or exiting the water from a boat.

hatch – a doorway on a boat.

helm – the location on a boat from which a boat is steered and controlled. May also be used to refer to who has control of the ship's wheel. See also bridge

head – the bathroom on the boat.

magnetometer – a device used to locate metal objects underwater.

mess – the room where meals are served.

metal detector – a hand-held device that is used to locate the presence of metals buried beneath sand, mud, or wrapped in marine growth.

penetratio n – the act of entering a shipwreck and moving beyond the zone where natural light provides illumination to see.

pilothouse – also known as "wheelhouse." Where the captain operates the boat from on a large boat.

port – as you face the front of the boat, the port side is to your left.

rail – the side of the boat.

RIB – stands for Rigid Inflatable Boat. An inflatable boat with a fiberglass deck and keel.

skipper – the captain of the ship.

side-scan sonar – a device that is towed behind a ship and used to record the topography of an underwater site.

starboard – as you face the front of the ship, the starboard side is to your right.

stern – The back end of the boat.

up-line – a reel and line that are used by a diver for the purpose of making an extended safety (or decompression) stop when there is no anchor line or decompression bar on which to hang. The line is attached to the bottom and the diver reels it out as he ascends to his stop depth.

wheelhouse – the cabin on the boat where the captain steers the ship

winch – a mechanical device used to raise and/or lower any heavy loads. The anchor may be raised by a winch designed specifically for this purpose.

© Bob Evans/La Mer Bleu

About the author - Steve Barsky

Steve Barsky started diving in 1965 in Los Angeles County, and became a diving instructor in 1970. His first employment in the industry was with a dive store in Los Angeles, and he went on to work for almost 10 years in the retail dive store environment.

Steve attended the University of California at Santa Barbara, where he earned a Masters Degree in 1976 in Human Factors/Ergonomics. This has helped greatly in his thorough understanding of diving equipment design and use. His master's thesis was one of the first to deal with the use of underwater video systems in commercial diving. His work was a pioneering effort at the time (1976) and was used by the Navy in developing applications for underwater video systems.

His background includes being a commercial diver, working in the offshore oil industry in the North Sea, Gulf of Mexico, and South America. He worked as both an air diving supervisor and a mixed gas saturation diver, making working dives down to 580'.

Barsky was marketing manager for Viking America, Inc., an international manufacturer of dry suits. He also served in a similar position at Diving Systems International (DSI), the world's leading manufacturer of commercial diving helmets.

Steve is an accomplished underwater photographer. His photos have been used in numerous magazine articles, catalogs, advertising, training programs, and textbooks.

A prolific writer, Barsky's work has been published in *Sea Technology*, *Skin Diver*, *Offshore Magazine*, *Emergency*, *Fire Engineering*, *Dive Training Magazine*, *Searchlines*, *Sources*, *Undersea Biomedical Reports*, *Santa Barbara Magazine*, *Underwater Magazine*, and many other publications. He is the author of the *Dry Suit Diving Manual*, *Diving in High Risk Environments*, *California Lobster Diving*, *Spearfishing for Skin and Scuba Divers*, *Small Boat Diving*, *Diving with the EXO-26 Full Face Mask*, *Diving with the Divator MK II Full Face Mask*, and a joint author with Dick Long and Bob Stinton of *Dry Suit Diving: A Guide to Diving Dry*. Steve has taught numerous workshops on contaminated water diving, dry suits, small boat diving, spearfishing, and other diving topics. *The Simple Guide to Rebreather Diving* was written by Steve along with Mark Thurlow and Mike Ward.

For Scuba Diving International, Steve has authored this book, as well as *Easy Nitrox Diving with Dive Computers. Night Diving, Underwater Navigation, and Limited Visibility Diving* is another title and *Deeper Sport Diving with Dive Computers* is also available.

In 1989 Steve formed Marine Marketing and Consulting, based in Santa Barbara, California. The company provides market research, marketing plans, consulting, newsletters, promotional articles, technical manuals, and other services for the diving and ocean industry. He has consulted to Dräger, AquaLung/U.S. Divers Co., Inc, Zeagle Systems, Inc., Light and Motion, Diving Unlimited Intnl., Kirby Morgan Diving Systems, DAN, NAUI, SSI, Viking, and numerous other companies.

He also investigates diving accidents and serves as an expert witness in dive accident litigation.

In 1999, Steve and his wife Kristine formed Hammerhead Press to publish high quality diving books. Hammerhead Press is a subsidiary of the Carcharodon Corporation.

Steve is an instructor with SDI, TDI, and other organizations. You can purchase Steve's other books at your local dive store, or on-line at http://www.hammerheadpress.com/

Index

E

F

T